*Five Keys to Unlocking
The Gift in the Wound*

FIVE KEYS TO UNLOCKING

THE GIFT IN THE WOUND

*The deeper the wound,
the greater the gift.*

MARK L. DAYTON

with

C. BRADFORD CHAPPELL, PhD

•

© 2018 Timpanogos Publishing, L.L.C.

Salt Lake City, Utah

Copyright © 2018 Timpanogos Publishing

All rights reserved. No part of this publication may be reproduced, distributed, or transmitted in any form or by any means, including photocopying, recording, or other electronic or mechanical methods, without the prior written permission of the publisher, except in the case of brief quotations embodied in critical reviews and certain other noncommercial uses permitted by copyright law. For permission requests, write to the publisher, addressed "Attention: Permissions Coordinator," at the address below.

Timpanogos Publishing
520 10th Avenue
Salt Lake City, UT 84103
www.timpanogospublishing.com

Ordering Information:

Quantity sales. Special discounts are available on quantity purchases by corporations, associations, and others. For details, contact the publisher at the address above.

Printed in the United States of America

ISBN 978-1-7322363-0-1

Cover art: Liam Lane
Editor: Jacob W. Dayton

First Edition

To my wife Cynthia, who has walked with me through my deepest wounds and patiently guided me to higher consciousness and joy than I ever imagined possible. Your vision inspired me beyond myself to share this journey and insight with others who may benefit. You are the greatest gift in my life.

To my talented editor (and son) Jacob for his perceptive insights and incorrigible grammatical correctness. I am deeply indebted to him for the hours we spent clarifying ideas and concept flow.

To my dear friend Brad whose wit and wisdom dispelled darkness with the light of truth and insight. Your gifts of militant healing and gift-in-the-wound enlightenment will bless countless generations in need of healing.

And most of all, to my higher power, through whom kernels of truth and clarity were distilled and woven into the fabric of my experience and expression. I am merely the messenger of His timeless truths that have been graciously shared for the benefit of all.

Table of Contents

Introduction

The Gift in the Wound 1

Prologue

The Wound 5

Section 1

The Pool We Swim In: How Did I Get Here? 15

Two Approaches 18

How's That Working For You? 26

How Did I Get Here? 35

Key 1 51

Choice: The First Great Principle 53

Key 2 63

Victory Over Victim: Dead Ends 65

Section 2

The Pool We Swim In: Paradox and the Linear Model 79

Paradox: The Second Great Principle 82

Two Views of Reality: Linear and Non-Linear 90

Key 3 105

Pain And The Purpose of Pain 107

The Pain Paradox 119

Militant Healing..135

Key 4..147

Gratitude... 149

Forgiveness 158

Key 5...167

Intuition, Not Effort 169

Create the Space.. 180

Section 3

The Pool We Swim In: Return to Wholeness 187

Epilogue

The Gift.. 199

Afterword

Wound to the Head... 203

Appendix

Bibliography... 214

About Mark L. Dayton..215

About C. Bradford Chappell, PhD 216

Everyone has a wound
Every wound has a gift

The deeper the wound
The greater the gift

Pain is the portal
To unlocking

The gift in the wound

INTRODUCTION
The Gift in the Wound

INTRODUCTION : THE GIFT IN THE WOUND

Each of us has gifts right in front of us, hidden in plain sight. Some of our greatest life-gifts are literally wrapped and locked up in front of us, and we never open them. In fact, we avoid them.

Ironically, the keys to unlock the gifts are also right in front of us, available to use at any time. But we believe them to be our enemy. We never get close to them, much less pick them up, insert them into the locks and turn to open the gifts. Instead, we avoid them like the plague.

If these gifts are so obvious, why don't we see them? Where are they hidden? Why don't we use them? The gifts reside within our emotional and psychological wounds. It's one of life's great paradoxes: our deepest wounds carry our greatest gifts. Gifts of insight, wisdom and understanding. Gifts of confidence, energy, power and motivation. Gifts of joy, serenity and peace.

It sounds so simplistic and obvious. Of course that would be the case. Many people say, "Oh, it's like life-lessons, or the moral of the story. Learning from our mistakes. That kind of thing." While those are valuable nuggets at one level, there is a deeper level that holds much deeper insight and wisdom buried within much deeper wounds. They are often illusive and annoyingly stubborn to access. Because of the deeper pain and suffering associated with these gifts, we've locked them away, and avoid dredging them up. It's simply our nature – we resist pain instinctively.

We all have wounds. Everyone has a wound. Every wound has a gift. The deeper the wound, the greater the gift. But we bury and lock the gifts deep within the wounds. They are there and available, if we will access the keys to turn the locks that reveal their valuable treasures.

And the keys? If they are also in plain sight, why don't we just pick them up and use them? The keys, paradoxically, are human qualities we also instinctively avoid because they cause us so much angst: choice, victim mindset, forgiveness, gratitude, and the most powerful of them all, pain itself. Putting these keys into the gift locks might seem simple and intuitive, but is actually counter to every natural human instinct we possess. Hence the paradox.

This book explores these five keys for unlocking our deepest, most meaningful life-gifts. The five keys provide insight and techniques into understanding our pain, understanding our wounds, and discovering how to effortlessly open and receive the gifts. The process is not painless, and runs counter to our instinctual programming, which is why so few people complete the journey. But it is ultimately effortless, joyful, and healing for those willing to fully engage.

I invite you on a journey of personal discovery through the pages of this book. It is based on the experiences of my own journey from deep depression and near-suicide to healing, joy and wholeness through discovering the gifts in deep wounding. It will guide you in understanding the five keys and how to apply them in unlocking your own hidden gifts, and getting past the blocks and barriers that are keeping you from achieving and receiving all that a rich life has to offer. You will also understand the key role played by guides and mentors in our lives who can make all the difference in our mindsets and healing.

The first section helps with understanding the emotional water we all swim in that filters the perceptions of our world and our wounding. This helps explain our blind spots and gain insights into wounds and pain that have been concealed and carried for many years that unconsciously affect how we operate in the world.

Section 2 explores the topic of paradox more deeply, and introduces a model for better understanding linear thinking vs. increasing our levels of consciousness. This is crucial in coming to our own resolution of the great paradox and dealing with the associated pain.

The final section completes the journey, bringing us back to the wholeness we can enjoy through discovering the gifts in our wounds. Receiving the gifts becomes effortless and freeing, allowing us to return to a sense of wholeness with which we first entered the world.

PROLOGUE
The Wound

PROLOGUE : THE WOUND

My world was spiraling out of control. For years I had been on a knife's edge between success and failure, and finally, I fell. Because of changes in the investor climate and obscure clauses in business contracts, my high-flying start-up failed, and with it went every single penny I had spent 20 years of a very successful business career saving up. I was bankrupt. I went from visions of cocktail parties and *Fortune* covers to nightmares of even being able to buy an issue of *Fortune*. Never did I expect to be facing total financial ruin.

But even worse was facing the investors, people who had shown such faith and excitement in our venture, and had provided the funding to get us off the ground and on a trajectory of high growth in a burgeoning new market. Among the shareholders were many friends and family whom I now avoided because I was so embarrassed. The one person my financial mismanagement had affected most was my wife, and I wished that I could somehow even hide from her.

The day I was summoned to appear in bankruptcy court was the most humiliating experience of my life.

I had heard about people wanting to put a paper bag over their heads at times like this, and had always thought it sounded a little weird. "It's just a few minutes in front of a judge in a room with a bunch of other strangers," I had thought. But standing there behind the bar, I understood to my very bones what those people must have been going through.

It's not the three minutes in front of the judge. It's the regret, the deep humiliation and the endless second-guessing: Why did I do that? Why didn't I see it coming? Why did she? How could I have been so blind? How could he do that? How could God let this happen? And on, and on, and on. It's the sleepless nights, the tortured days, and the hope ebbing out with each new setback. It's a wound that never heals, but continues to fester and ooze.

At least, that's how I saw it. And though the moment did pass, the effects lingered on. Soon enough, I found myself spiraling into uncontrollable depression. I tried everything I could think of to combat this feeling. I read countless books and diligently tried to implement their suggestions. I would get on a new program, get excited about setting a new direction, then charge off on another quest. With each one I was sure change was just around the corner. After a few weeks of pushing through, I was hanging on by sheer willpower and still not feeling the underlying shift in my attitude or outlook. Then, invariably, something would come along that would push me backward: a job interview that didn't go well, a friend or family member who had something great come into their life, unexpected bills or expenses that squeezed us even tighter, or goals and schedules that never seemed to be within reach. Bit by bit the light would fade, and I'd find myself back in the same dark world.

Next I tried the medication route. I scheduled an appointment with a doctor I knew, to see if an exam would turn up anything out of the ordinary. I've always been quite healthy, so I wasn't surprised when following the visit, the results turned up no pathology that was out of the normal range. In fact, like most previous exams, the lab values were in the range normally seen in men 10 years my junior. "You must be a runner or marathoner," the doctor suggested. "No, just naturally lean with low heart rate," I replied.

With no particular pathology to point to, the doctor suggested I try a mild anti-depressant. Even though I grew up in a medical family, I normally don't like taking pills. But I was desperate enough to try nearly anything at this point, so I started the trial regimen.

PROLOGUE : THE WOUND

I'm very committed to things I put my mind to, so sticking with the prescribed dosages wasn't a problem. But after several weeks, I didn't see any difference in my mood or outlook, and I was tiring of the "buzzed" feeling the medication produced. More discouraged than ever, I continued my search for answers.

My religious advisor suggested a counselor who might be able to help me work through some of my issues and find answers. I set up an appointment and began twice-weekly sessions. At first our discussions were helpful, and our visits gave me something positive to look forward to. We began exploring various issues and options, and I worked on the homework he suggested. But over time, I began to have that "stuck" feeling again. It was like I had gotten off to a good start, got my hopes up that I was making real progress, only to find myself bogging down again in fear, frustration and hopelessness.

The next stage of the journey took me to holistic healing, where I tried a variety of different natural remedies combined with strict attention to a healthy, balanced diet, and regular exercise. Of everything I had tried, this seemed to help the most. As long as I was diligent, my mood at least stayed out of the danger zone. But over time, as I would feel my mood lightening, I felt as though I was constantly bumping up against a glass ceiling that kept me and my dark moods from rising any higher. I felt stuck just "getting by".

Well-meaning people told me, "There's a lesson in there somewhere for you. Just hang on." But I couldn't imagine there was real meaning in all this. Why me? Why had my dreams and expectations evaporated? Why not for others? I was sure there was more to life than merely going through it. I could see others around me who seemed genuinely happy and fulfilled. But, try as I might, I couldn't seem to rise above the subsistence level of emotional health.

Almost as emotionally draining as my futile healing attempts were the monthly trips to my dear parent's home for money to see us through with the essentials while I was looking for a job. Each time my mom handed me a check I would assure her I was searching as hard as possible, and that a good job was bound to come up soon. But if my words sounded anything like the feeling of despair in my heart, it probably wasn't overly convincing. And based on the number of job offers coming in, I wasn't exactly hitting it out of the park with potential employers.

To top it off, my marriage was falling apart. My cherished wife of nearly than 25 years, Cynthia, had reached the end of her rope in trying to hold together a relationship increasingly devoid of caring, understanding, and partnership. I had become bitter and hopeless, and it increasingly fell to my wife to hold the family together. She did everything she could while I slipped further and further into my lonely, dark hole.

On good days, as I was driving to my odd-job consulting appointments I would see a school crossing guard or lawn trimmer at work and think, "I could do that. That wouldn't be so bad."

On bad days, I would have been fine with just ending it all. A number of times, as I stood at a busy intersection waiting to cross the street I thought, "It would be super easy to just step out in front of that car or semi, and then this would all be over. It would probably be better for everyone anyway. I'm causing so many people so much pain. The world would be better off without me." On those days, all that stood between me and taking that step was the fleeting flicker of my family's apparent desire to still have me around.

PROLOGUE : THE WOUND

The Line

Finally, one day Cynthia drew the line in the sand.

The years of depression, victimization, and career suicide had pushed her to the point of losing hope of ever resuscitating our relationship. We went for a walk and she outlined the options. "I've been talking to a friend about our situation, and she's been working with a counselor for a number of years who she says is fantastic for helping people like us. But it has to be us – you and me. There's no solo option in this. I've set up an appointment for next week for the two of us. If you're not in, I'm out."

I got the message. I didn't expect that this counselor would be any different than the last, but for the sake of saving our marriage I agreed to give it a shot.

First Impressions

The next week we went to the office and were ushered in to meet Brad. He greeted us warmly and directed us to a couch facing his chair.

The first things that struck me were his kindly face, the slight twinkle in his eye, and a wry smile that suggested meaningful conversation mixed with playful humor.

He was dressed in a crisp, starched shirt, jeans, and cowboy boots. I started to get this picture of a juxtaposition between country ruggedness and cultural refinement. Although he was a little informal and at times brusque, I immediately felt comfortable and safe around him.

He proceeded to tell us a little about his approach: He accepted traditional concepts of psychology, but focused on transformation and healing rather than curing, and described this approach through the analogy of a caterpillar transforming from its original state to cocoon to butterfly. That motif of metamorphosis was on his business card, website, and some of the items in his office.

Particularly striking was a picture in the entry depicting each stage of the metamorphosis in succession along a long horizontal twig stretching across the frame. On the far left was the caterpillar, and on the far right, the fully emerged adult monarch butterfly, with each stage of the transformation superimposed on the twig in between. It was a striking image that caught my attention when I first entered the office. I tried not to take Brad's analogy too literally, but if forced to choose I would probably say I was feeling more caterpillar than butterfly at this particular moment.

Beyond the analogy, I wasn't sure I understood the difference or the significance between healing and curing, but I was liking much of what I had heard so far. That said, as he spoke there were still a few questions in my mind.

Over the course of our conversation, Brad shared some things that gave me the clear impression that this man was speaking from experience, from having been there and lived this transformational journey – like he had actually walked the path I was on, and maybe more. I didn't get the impression this was textbook theory, but sound, lasting principles refined in the crucible of experiential fire.

Speaking of PhDs, he didn't dwell on degrees, prestigious graduate programs, or national recognitions, (all of which he had), but rather spoke with some feeling about what he referred to as "the cancer group." Although he had never dealt with cancer, some 20 years

PROLOGUE : THE WOUND

earlier Brad had started this group as an attempt to help a person or two dealing with terminal cancer diagnoses find meaning and closure in life. Before long it evolved into a larger group of ardent cancer copers and survivors, many of whom had defied terminal diagnoses and lived well beyond any medical expectations. Brad hinted at the strong connection between our minds and bodies, and the ultimate power we have to choose.

I could sense we were winding up the introductions and transitioning to the part where I had to talk. I took out a notepad and pen and prepared to jot a few notes from our conversation. Over the years I learned that I'm a somewhat rare blend of a written and visual learner. When I'm trying to absorb new material or insights, I take fairly detailed notes of things that strike me, and that I want to remember. Unlike some people I know, I can read my own handwriting later, and I actually do go back and review the notes and refresh my memory on the ideas that jumped out at me.

My visual side also manifests itself in this process, and I find myself sketching little diagrams or pictures that enhance and illustrate the conversations. They serve as little memory-joggers that connect dots in my thinking and learning. I'm not an artist, by any stretch. But my illustrations help me focus on the simple, central ideas that underlie most new concepts.

I got a sense that I would be discovering some new concepts with this coach that I'd want to hold onto. So with pen and pad at the ready, I made my first entries:

Notes From My Note Pad

First Meeting With Brad

> Transformation and healing vs. curing – I like the metamorphosis analogy, but I think it runs deeper than what we discussed today
>
> Experience vs. theory – he seems to have walked the walk

SECTION 1
The Pool We Swim In: How Did I Get Here?

SECTION 1 : THE POOL WE SWIM IN: HOW DID I GET HERE?

Before exploring the keys to discovering the gift in the wound, it's important to step back and first understand where we currently are from a consciousness or awareness standpoint, and how we got here at this point in time. With that foundation, we can better navigate our way forward along the path of discovery.

There is a story of two young fish swimming along who happen to meet an older fish swimming in the opposite direction. The older fish nods at them and says in passing, "Morning, boys. How's the water?" The two young fish swim on for a bit, and then eventually one looks over at the other and says, "What is he talking about? What's water?"

Often, when we are in the thick of things, and life with all its challenges is coming at us fast, we have little or no awareness of the emotional framework we filter all of our life experiences through. It's often called "the water we swim in", our own personal swimming pool that is made up of the experiences, beliefs, perceptions – and especially the wounds – we accumulated in our early years, often from those who cared for us and loved us most.

We are mostly unaware of this emotional filter surrounding us and heavily influencing how we perceive and relate to the relationships and experiences in our world.

This first section overviews three key concepts that are fundamental to formulating our personal emotional swimming pool:

- Our misperception that we are somehow broken and need to be fixed, when in reality we are each whole and complete, but with an incomplete understanding or consciousness of our status.

- Our stories, and how we tend to get "stuck in the story" of our perceived situation in life.

- The pervasive influence that our socialization or domestication had on creating our perceptual waters.

We'll then jump into the first two keys: Choose, and Victory Over Victim. These two keys set the stage for understanding the power of the additional keys that will open the door to our deepest wounds and greatest gifts.

SECTION 1 : TWO APPROACHES

Two Approaches

The realization that we are both completely insignificant and vitally important gives us the perspective to see that every experience in life is perfect, as are we.

Well, let's talk about your situation, Brad began.

"Before we jump in, I have a couple of questions for you," I said.

Okay, shoot.

"I've worked with a number of different professionals, and your approach seems quite different."

Well, like many of my good colleagues, I was trained in classical, linear psychology. I received a PhD in social psychology and for 25 years I worked with patients from that framework. My job was to assess, diagnose and treat. And after 25 years I found I wasn't helping nearly as much as I'd like, and yet people were still coming to me and paying me money for therapy. I became convinced there had to be a better way.

As I thought it through, I decided I had the model backwards. That approach always starts with a diagnosis. It basically says, "You have this problem, we're going to label it xyz, and then we'll fix it." That model works pretty well in the world of physical ailments, but in my world of psychology this starting premise is all wrong.

When we diagnose and label someone with a psychological or emotional challenge, we're saying, "You're broken. You're defective as a human being. And I know how to fix you." For the vast majority of human beings, I don't believe that assesment to be true. I believe we are all perfect individuals with imperfect awareness or understanding.

"Perfect?" I queried." You don't really mean perfect, do you?"

The majority of us traversing life on this planet spend a good part of that existence believing we are somehow defective, separate, and that we have lost something. It's true that we have flaws. All creatures do. I discovered that it's this imperfect understanding of ourselves that gets in the way of the healing journey. So my challenge from the beginning is to help people believe that they aren't broken, or defective, but that they are perfect, with perfect flaws that need to be viewed from a different level of understanding.

With that as a starting point, we can then work together to discover the truth within that is at the core of healing. It's a discovery, or return to who you really are, not fixing something that was broken – which in reality wasn't really broken in the first place.

So, to answer your original question, the difference in my approach is that I consider myself more of a coach than a therapist. Rather than diagnose and treat, which would be the curing approach, I coach you through the transformation of self-discovery that is at the core of healing.

I was working hard to understand what he was telling me. "So most of us believe we are somehow broken, and lacking?" I probed further.

Remembered Wholeness

There is something in each one of us that has a need to be loved, and that sense makes us feel as if we existed before coming to this earth. It is what has been called remembered wholeness. Something in us remembers a connectedness. It's common to all human beings, regardless of religious, ethnic, or cultural background. It's an idea that runs through almost every tradition, theology and philosophy. Almost universally our cultures are filled with this theme: songs, stories, books, movies, fairy tales, oral histories, and lore portray the cycle of birth and death and the theme of a journey back home. These ideas resonate deeply at a basic level that we really can't explain. Within us is a desire to go back to where we came from. We long for home. We have a longing to be ourselves and to be loved for who we are. Ultimately, these feelings penetrate to the deepest personal level – into the heart.

This sense seems to predate our mortal birth and often creates a tension in us that starts us searching for this perceptional lost past. We have deep remembering of it. There is something within us that recalls belonging to something greater than ourselves. It is this remembered wholeness that motivates us to search for that which we believe we have lost.

But these feelings of separation are more than the wishful hoping of our heart. They represent an often-unacknowledged truth that our essence truly did begin before this life. When we accept that fact, we experience the sensation that somehow, we have returned home. It's not a return to a physical wholeness. Rather, it's a return to a sense of wholeness, that we're not somehow inherently defective. We begin to sense that we're perfect creations of a perfect universe and of a perfect god.

> That goes against every linear, ego thought process that we have been socialized with.

"Linear? Socialized?" I thought. "What does he mean?" Brad continued.

> On the other hand, the notion of being imperfect, or being flawed, is part of a spell that is cast on every single person who comes into the world during the domestication or socialization process as we were growing up. However, the sense of remembered wholeness never leaves us. It can be battered, it can be covered with layers of pain and heartache, and it sometimes can literally be forgotten. But it is always there when we can silence the cluttered mind.
>
> Are your ready for a little homework?

"Sure. What do you have in mind?"

> On a still, dark night, go outside, get away from city lights, and look up at the heavens. As you view the stars, you are literally looking back in time billions of years. In all that space, you are pretty insignificant. You aren't even a dust particle, relatively speaking. Yet, in all that space, there is no one exactly like you. You are absolutely unique in all the universe. That boggles the mind. And rightly so, because in that moment you are facing one of life's great paradoxes.
>
> You are both significant and insignificant. How can this be?
>
> For people who live by the ocean, here's another interesting paradoxical experiment. Take a walk on the beach. Find a quiet place and scoop up a handful of sand. You might say

SECTION 1 : TWO APPROACHES

sand is sand – it all looks the same. But one handful of sand contains approximately 400,000 grains of sand.[1] Put it under a microscope, and you discover a myriad of different sizes, shapes and colors. In fact, scientists tell us that as far as we can tell, no two grains of sand are the same in the world. That is a mindboggling concept, and yet we know that each grain is totally unique.

Brad pulled out a folder with microscope photographs of sand grains from different beaches from around the world. Each was unique and strangely beautiful.

So grains of sand are completely insignificant parts of a vast shoreline, and yet at the same time completely unique and fascinating.

"Wow, that's really interesting," I stated. "I honestly had never considered that before, and I think I get the parallel between us and the sand," I said as I cleared my throat. "But honestly Brad, whether I'm sand, star, or snowflake it's not very helpful when my life is falling apart."

Point well taken, but had you considered that your falling apart might be linked to your understanding of you? It's not just that you are unique. That's only half the story. The other half is that you are also insignificant. As humans, we have a hard time holding those two thoughts simultaneously in our minds, so we tend to default to the one that is more believable: that we are insignificant. And that's a lie – one of the most damaging lies of humanity, because it causes us to lose sight of the vision of our greatness and potential.

Until you resolve that paradox, you are doomed to live the lie of insignificance.

"Hmmm…Okay, so, do you want to coach me through this paradox thing?" I returned.

> All in good time. Right now, here's another way to think about it: Everything that exists in this universe has a purpose. Conversely, if something doesn't have a purpose in the universe, it doesn't exist. Everything that has structure has a function. All things are purposeful. Therefore, you have a purpose because you exist. You are purposeful, no matter how small or insignificant you may seem. Because this cannot be proven scientifically, you must choose to believe this principle of purpose.
>
> On the physical level, you may have one leg shorter than another, you may have a genetic predisposition to a physical disorder, you may have diabetes, or you may be mentally retarded, but you are still whole and perfect. When you get really quiet and in touch with sensory experiences, all people instinctively know they are perfect because they remember their ancient connection with wholeness, that feeling of pre-existence, of coming home.

The conversation was getting a little beyond me. "So, back to the homework. Does it require a write-up or something about my experience?" I queried.

> Maybe a journal entry after your experience. As you practice taking quiet moments to ponder, over time you will begin to sense a greater purpose in your life. Maybe some new insights that you hadn't previously noticed or understood will come to you, or maybe you will simply feel that connection to remembered wholeness. Either way, you will feel something beyond yourself telling you about yourself.

SECTION 1 : TWO APPROACHES

You see, purpose can't be thought, studied, or planned. It's not like writing a mission statement for your life. It can only be sensed. It can only be remembered in the sacred moments of quietude, when something ancient speaks to our heart. If night and stars don't work for you, sit by a stream, go for a long walk in a quiet place, or find a place of solitude where you can connect.

"It sounds a bit mystical," I said. "I don't have to sit in a yoga pose or anything, right?"

Whatever allows you to clear your mind and listen to your heart, your inner voice. Sometimes it takes great courage to follow that voice, and it certainly takes time, patience and perseverance. But despite the level of effort it requires, I have never known anyone who has done this inner work who looked back with regret. Most often it is when we don't listen to our heart that we have regrets.

If you are willing, and choose to make the effort, it will be a deeply meaningful and unique experience. I'm sure of it. It will help you stay present. You'll start remembering who you really are.

"I hope so. There hasn't been much meaningful going on in my life lately," I returned.

It will be the perfect experience, because every experience is the perfect experience.

"Every experience?" I asked.

Yes. But that's a discussion for another time. In the meantime, you've got some stargazing to do.

Notes From My Note Pad

We aren't broken or defective; We are all perfect individuals with imperfect awareness or understanding.

He's a coach: doesn't diagnose and fix; helps you return to who you really are.

Sense of remembered wholeness never leaves us.

Paradox: you are both significant and insignificant (stars; grains of sand); as humans, we tend to mostly believe we are insignificant.

Homework: star or sand gazing

Pictures From My Sketch Pad

◯

WHOLENESS

SECTION 1 : HOW'S THAT WORKING FOR YOU?

How's That Working For You?

Having a wound, even one we're not aware of, is one of life's greatest opportunities for growth.

I was looking forward to our next meeting, as I hoped we would be able to dive into my issues and really get down to the business of fixing my problems.

As Brad greeted me, I was struck again at the odd juxtaposition of his crisp, businesslike demeanor and his warm, natural manner. After some friendly chatter, he invited me to start by telling him more details about my situation. With relish, I dove into all the awful things that had happened to me over the past several years: Brutus-like business partners, bankruptcy, toxic relationships, humiliation, depression, and a horde of other terrible events.

> I paused momentarily, expecting maybe some empathic affirmations or reflective feedback before I continued. Brad stopped for a minute, leaned forward and said, So, how's that working for you?

I came within an inch of jumping up off the couch and punching him in the face. I'm not a violent man, but I had never wanted to hit someone so badly. I was furious. I thought, "Are you kidding? I just spilled my guts to you about how awful things are in my life, and you have the gall to ask how it's working for me? Isn't that fairly obvious?"

Through a tightly clenched jaw I sarcastically blurted out, "It's not working at all, obviously."

> Sensing my level of agitation, Brad offered, You just shared with me your story about how you've been wounded by different people and circumstances in your life. We all have stories we hold onto that define us and our reality. They are usually rooted in pain and fear, and a lot of misperceptions, but we use them to define who and why we are. In essence, it's being 'stuck in the story.'

Not much of that made sense to me. I was still fighting my first impulse to walk out before I did something drastic. But part of me was intrigued to understand what he was saying, so after cooling down a bit, I decided to stick it out a bit longer.

"Okay, so what do you mean, my story?" I offered. "I didn't come here to tell stories. I came here to get out of this hole I'm in." Brad sat back a said, Let me give you an example.

> Some twenty-five years ago a young woman was referred to me because, in addition to having an inoperable brain tumor, she had been diagnosed with depression. But in contrast to her diagnoses, as I worked with her, I witnessed her grace and dignity as she faced one dismal prognosis after another. This young lady had just gotten married and was starting a new chapter in her life, but rather than curse circumstance, resist her fate, and wallow in justifiable misery, she chose to accept her sorry situation and put forth her best face. One could almost see the transcendent peace within her.

> Her husband however, never was able to accept the terminality of her condition. His hopes and dreams were shattered by her

diagnosis. With each failure by science, he became more and more frantic. He latched on to every rumor of a miracle cure and begged her to try it.

She, however, had no desire to try these things. Unlike her husband, she was completely at peace with her diagnosis. She was calm and resigned, he wasn't. She was victimized by her cancer but not the victim, whereas he had completely submitted himself to the awful reign of her diagnosis.

Much like him, I did not want to admit that death was inevitable, even though in my heart I knew it to be so. I saw death as failure. That perception kept me from being present. Her husband's grief and anxiety kept him from being present. Since that time I have come to understand that being present is very much part of the healing process. Life is sacred and most people do not want to die. But death comes to us all, so we have not failed because we die. Failure may be that while alive we never really chose to live. In the end, I think we both failed her.

This young woman and many since have taught me that when we lose something we love or experience something that causes pain in our lives, it creates a wound. Dealing with this woman helped me realize that everyone has a wound. But, there is a gift in every wound, and the deeper the wound, the greater the gift. *Healing is the process of finding the gift in the wound.*

And healing, as this young woman demonstrated, brings transcendent joy. But it is a choice. It doesn't just happen. Unfortunately, the vast majority of those who walk this earth choose the easier route of remaining in and defending stories, vainly hoping for some miracle cure.

If you are expecting that I will cure or fix your problems, you are going to be sorely disappointed. Actually, there isn't an effective way to cure or fix you. Rather, you must undertake a healing journey – a journey of discovering your own answers, direction, and peace; of finding the gift in the wound.

Our wounds are all unique, and uniquely matched to us and our needs and opportunities for healing and raising our level of consciousness. The key is to have faith that despite the pain, there is still beauty to be found.

"Okay…." I said, trying to process these half-formed, foggy ideas in my mind.

"You said everyone has a wound. For some people, that's fairly obvious, looking at the challenges they face in life. But I know people who seem to be doing just fine. They may have minor setbacks, but for the most part, their lives seem to be pretty much wound-free. They have great jobs, happy families, plenty of money, seem to get along great with everyone. Where's the wound in that?" I pressed.

Every life journey is unique to that individual, and uniquely suited to providing the experiences matched to their needs. Wounds can come to us in many ways and timeframes, and can manifest burdens we carry, but of which we may not be consciously unaware.

There was a woman who carried this type of burden. She got a good education, had wonderful friends, and a fulfilling job working as a nutritionist in a hospital. Her life seemed to be going perfectly. She was active in her church and volunteer projects, went on fun trips with friends, and enjoyed a variety of artistic outlets.

SECTION 1 : HOW'S THAT WORKING FOR YOU?

One day she was in a hospital room and stopped for a minute to watch a segment of a TV program the patient had playing. The report was talking about children who had been abused in some manner in their younger lives and had repressed and completely blocked out the memory of the incidents, only to have them resurface much later in their lives as adults.

She said as she stood there watching the report, an overwhelming feeling hit her: "That's me." As she processed that feeling over the next weeks and months, she came to realize that she had been raised in a severely abusive environment that had affected her deeply.

She discovered a wound she was completely oblivious to. The ensuing pain was so intense that it required many months to find meaning and purpose in the dark and sordid affronts to her innocence.

In perhaps a less dramatic way, we have all been wounded in our upbringing by someone in our families. This is almost always completely unintentional, administered by people who love and care for us. But in the process of growing up, we are inculcated with ideas and beliefs that aren't entirely true, and that set us up for pain and challenges later on. Most people discover that in one way or another, they carry a wound from their upbringing that affects their view of and approach to life, often in very limiting and frustrating ways. At the appropriate time in your journey we'll explore this domestication, or socialization process.

Other types of wounds are carried, but willfully ignored or justified. I know many people, for example, who struggle with a family or other close relationship that is less than ideal to the point that they don't even speak to or associate with the person. Often they will say they are fine with things as they are, or justify the current state of affairs by saying something like, "It's just the way it goes in life. We really have nothing to talk about, and we are so far apart, there is no way we will ever repair this relationship."

They deal with the pain by avoiding the person or the relationship, pushing it out of their minds and lives. But the wound is still there, regardless of whether it is ignored or denied. While it may be true that the relationship can't be improved or repaired, based on the other person's choice, the pain of the wound is still unresolved. This is the type of person who will tell you everything is just fine, but deeper down, there is a simmering unacknowledged trauma.

Though it's a rare circumstance, there actually are people for whom everything has gone ideally. There is nothing wrong with that, but at some point, even they will face wounding to one degree or another. We will all lose a loved one to death, be touched by illness or tragedy, or be faced with circumstances we are unable to explain. Wounding is an integral and essential part of human experience.

Many people go to great lengths to avoid any type of wounding and opposition in life. While I don't recommend going out looking for trouble, finding healing through leaning into painful experiences always results in a much deeper, fuller life experience made sweeter with the wisdom and indescribable joy that accompanies a raised level of consciousness.

As Brad paused, I summarized out loud the note I was scribbling. "So each wound bears the gift of understanding a life lesson. Isn't that what we usually call character building experiences?"

SECTION 1 : HOW'S THAT WORKING FOR YOU?

Actually, it's much more than that. While painful experiences can and do teach valuable lessons, finding the gift in the wound goes much deeper. Building character might include asking "What did I learn from that?" or "What's the moral of the story?", but healing is a truly transformative journey that shifts our perception of reality at our deepest level and ushers in peace and joy.

Brad looked up at the clock. I was surprised to see that our time was up. As I gathered my things, Brad said, "Thanks for not punching me earlier. I saw you fighting to stay on the couch. I think we really hit a nerve."

I managed to muster a weak smile.

"That's good," he said as he slapped my back. "Means you're awake and willing to consider change. That's the essential foundation for making any progress. It just hurts like hell in the meantime," he replied with a wry smile as we walked out of his office.

Notes From My Note Pad

When we lose something we love/experience pain, it creates a wound.

The wound carries an opportunity for a gift.

Healing is the process of finding the gift in the wound.

Healing transcends curing, fixing, learning, and figuring it out. It's a transformation at the sensory or level.

Wounds can come to us in many ways and timeframes, or can manifest burdens we may carry, but are consciously unaware of (woman in the hospital)

Some wounds are carried, but largely ignored or justified.

Wound gifts aren't merely, "What did you learn from this experience," or "the moral of the story is…". They are transformative journeys that shift consciousness and perception of reality at the heart level = healing and transcendent joy.

So many good quotes – I'm starting a quote book page

Quotes From My Quote Book

Everyone has a wound.
Every wound has a gift   .
The deeper the wound the greater the gift.

SECTION 1 : HOW'S THAT WORKING FOR YOU?

Pictures From My Sketch Pad

WOUND

How Did I Get Here?

Our development, no matter how carefully overseen, has left us with deeply engrained and often negative beliefs about ourselves and the world around us.

My previous meeting with Brad really got my mind going with a flood of new ideas. After mulling things for more than a week, I could hardly wait to sit down and continue our discussion.

As I arrived for the next visit, I sat down in his office and launched right into it.

"I was thinking about what you said about the wounds we carry, especially the ones dealt to us by our caregivers and those who love us as we are growing up. I understand that this is mostly unintentional, but the more I thought about it, the more agitated I got. No, actually, I was really angry," I began.

"At first I was angry that I was angry. That turned to anger that I had to be going through this whole thing in the first place. The pain, the wounding, the anger. I realized that much of what I was dealing with was as a result of experiences I had growing up, and the attitudes and beliefs I developed in my own home.

"I was very angry with my parents. It didn't seem fair. I looked around at other people I know and many seem to have grown up in relatively idyllic situations, and as a result, don't have to deal with all the issues I do.

"Look, I love my parents. They're great people. I appreciate much of what they provided for me during my formative years. In many ways, I had a great life growing up. I mean, they didn't abuse me, they provided a comfortable home and surroundings, and they gave me a solid moral and religious founding and opportunities for developing my talents. But, there were some highly dysfunctional dynamics that so deeply affected me I've never been able to get past them and reach my full capabilities.

"It's not right, and it's not fair. Why do I have to deal with all this stuff that seems to always block my path? It seems like I take one step forward and two steps back."

Hmmm, Brad mused. Before we get into your specific issues, let's take a step back and explore how you got here. That might help give it some helpful perspective.

"Whatever you say," I responded, flipping open my notepad.

Okay, let's start where we all began: at birth.

Domestication & Socialization: Casting the Spell

All life begins with a connection. It always takes two elements – male and female, positive and negative, and biological and spiritual. As human beings we are connected first physically, then spiritually, then emotionally, and finally, psychologically. Throughout our life cycle we never lose the need for connection at all of those levels.

Birth begins a process of separation, of leaving, or of moving apart. This begins our journey into spiritual, emotional, and psychological separation. The parent-child connection, that symbiotic relationship, needs to be separate, or, like in any symbiotic relationship, they both die. Our socialization, or domestication as it is often referred to, is the process that initiates and defines this separation. It comes to all of us as part of growing and maturing in the familial, social, religious, and environmental situations we are born into. There is never a time in this process that the individual does not need to be a part of the larger social environment. We are social beings. We are hard-wired to be connected.

We don't come into this world with a sense of self. We are whole but have no sense of that wholeness. Our sense of self develops through our relationships to significant others, mainly parents, family, friends, and those closest to us. Those interactions begin the socialization or domestication journey.

As we mature psychologically, we develop a sense of self separate from the rest of world. We define this as ego. In fact, the purpose of the ego is to let us know that we are not something else. This is extremely important for survival. If a child does not know he is not the swimming pool or the road or the edge of the roof, very bad things can happen.

The ego develops to keep us safe. However, it sometimes does its job too well and tries to protect us from things that are not physically dangerous, such as someone's disapproval of us. While it hurts us emotionally, it is not dangerous to our physical person. This type of reaction by the ego to information or situations is the root of so many issues related to our domestication.

Everything in our psychology tells us we are separate from everything else. But this separateness feels threatening.

SECTION 1 : HOW DID I GET HERE?

Our sense of self is wired into our subconscious in relation to all other significant relationships and comes from how those that we have significant relationships with treat themselves and how they relate to us. The child takes on the sentiments of the parents and other important figures in their life. People often find themselves thinking and feeling about themselves the same way their parents thought and felt about themselves. People often motivate themselves the same way their parents motivated themselves.

The brain records all this data. A child's brain is recording all information about how their significant others think of them. As we continue through the separation cycle, our perceived separation is amplified by experiences we interpret to be about us, such as disapproval, neglect, or withdrawal of love. If the child believes the parent loves them, the child thinks, 'I am loveable,' and that identity starts to develop. But if a parent doesn't love him or herself, they will actually teach the child not to love themselves. The child doesn't have the ability to think that there may be something wrong with daddy. The child grows up believing they are unlovable - and that's an error. That's the spell that is cast on the child.

Every child is narcissistic, and that's why this spell works. They are narcissistic in the sense that when things happen outside of them, they think it means something about them. It's not until the child reaches the second decade of life that they can start to understand and think abstractly enough to think, 'Nothing that happens around me actually means anything about me except that I might have been there.' But there is a lot of corrupted data that has already been wired into the brain that leads the person to personalize events that in reality mean nothing about them.

"So, it makes sense that my parents and caregivers didn't intentionally try to plant erroneous ideas in my mind," I mused. "They aren't that way. But it's obvious that I learned some very destructive patterns and perceptions as part of the process. How does that happen?"

> We do not wire our brains consciously. Our *brain* wires what we eventually come to call us. As we become conscious of ourselves we can rewire the brain by choosing attitudes and beliefs.
>
> The nature of relationships are wired in the brain much like the nature of language. Children don't consciously know they are learning a language; the brain simply wires what it is exposed to. The same is true of relationships and a child's perception of self. This wiring takes place initially at the subconscious level, so neither the child nor the parents are aware the lessons they are teaching or receiving about relationships and self-perception. The child is unaware, and the parents are merely dong the best they can.
>
> If ideas and paradigms are not examined, old levels of consciousness get passed on from the parents. It's not a conscious process, its subconscious. But that's where the spell starts to get cast, passing on the belief that 'I am what you think I am.'

"But my parents were good people. They taught me values, hard work, responsibility, and service," I interjected.

> Originally most of what the brain learns is not what it hears, but what it senses. Children can sense safety and security long before they are capable of conscious thought. Because of this, our behavior is based more on what *wasn't* said to us than what *was* said to us.

If a parent shows attention and is present for the child, they are communicating, 'You are important to me; I believe in you.' The child is not hearing that consciously, but the brain is recording that data.

It's the subtle, indirect communication - what is not said - that the brain records. What is not said is communicated in body language, tone of the voice, the way the words are presented. It's the sensory experience.

The child just senses that the parent is disappointed or unhappy, and the child believes that means something about them. While there are some parents who call their children stupid or dumb, most children simply don't believe it. They say that can't be true - because it's direct. The more subtle the invalidation of the child, the deeper the impact on the subconscious and eventually on the self-esteem of the person.

More often than not, all the well-meaning people in our lives helped build our story, helped wire our beliefs about ourselves. Most of these beliefs are just not true, but we hold onto them, believing they reflect who we are.

Later in life we can examine the language as well at the relationships of these beliefs, and make changes or learn new languages or new ways of relating.

"Wow, I had no idea of the extent that I sponged up all the non-verbal cues that shaped my world and built my beliefs," I said." It's amazing how pervasive those experiences are for so many years into our future lives."

It is a lifelong journey to discover all our habits of domestication, Brad replied. Healing shame can be one of the most challenging aspects of that journey.

Shame

We all have made mistakes. Mistakes are those experiences that let us know what works and what doesn't. We gain wisdom from mistakes if and when we do not withdraw approval from ourselves. When mistakes become personal, that is, we define ourselves in terms of the mistake, we feel the sentiment of shame. Shame is the process of inherently withdrawing approval of ourselves – thereby creating a deep existential anxiety.

We are hard-wired biologically for approval. We need approval from our mortal care takers in childhood and in adulthood from spouses, children, friends, and significant others. Ultimately, we look for approval from whatever higher power we have come to believe in, even if that higher power is man-made or earth-bound. Without approval and love, we as a species just do not thrive. While we do not need to be loved by everyone, we do need to be loved by someone, and especially by ourselves.

It seems our ability to love and accept ourselves as human beings comes in a large degree from how much our early care-takers loved and approved of themselves. Being able to love themselves, they were able to love and accept us as human.

"So let me get this straight. My parents' love and acceptance of themselves had more of an impact on me than their love and acceptance of me? That seems backwards," I suggested.

It is highly counterintuitive. It seems that we would develop our own love of self based upon our early caretakers' love of us. But, the more powerful influence is based upon how much they loved *themselves*. Parents who love themselves are comfortable with who they are, and are therefore not threatened by a child who is pursuing their own individuality and exceptionalism. Unfortunately, the opposite is also true, and is generally the rule more than the exception.

Over the years I have observed many who carried the shame of their caretakers. This shame was passed on mostly unintentionally by very well-meaning people who for various reasons believed that some aspect of their humanness was unacceptable, and therefore they became unworthy of love, feeling somehow not worthwhile.

This inherently shows up or is intensified as a child in their life pursues his or her own individuality and makes what are considered to be 'mistakes,' or actions outside of expected norms. Besides violating cultural, religious or tradition-based boundaries, this could include pursuing paths and achieving success that threaten the parent's own sense of accomplishment and worth. Rather than being viewed for what they truly are – actions outside the parents' comfort zone – in the consciousness of the child, these experiences are perceived as not, 'I made a mistake,' but, 'I *am* the mistake.'

The key is to understand that the *love of self* is the keystone to healing all other relationships. This love heals the deep existential fear and sadness that come from the misinterpreted sentiment that one is a mistake. Marianne Williamson's now famous line, "It is our light, not our darkness that most frightens us" has been wonderfully inspirational for many people seeking to accept and love themselves for their true inherent gifts. However, at the same time it is a sad commentary on how a distorted perception of self has become true for so many.

My head was pounding with so many new ideas I thought it was going to explode. I was so focused I had even stopped writing. As I thought about my own family situation, I realized that Brad's explanation fit perfectly . My parents were kind, attentive, caring people who showed me a great amount of love, and yet their lack of self-confidence and acceptance of themselves had a great impact on my perception of my own capabilities and worth.

The more I thought about it, the more it made sense – even the counterintuitive parts. But that glimmer of understanding hadn't done a lot to calm the pain and anger that this whole domestication experience had caused in my life.

"Okay. I think I'm beginning to get it up here," I said, tapping my temple. "But here," hitting my chest with my fist, "is still undone. It's another one of those, 'easy to say, excruciatingly hard to do' quests. How do I just start loving myself more?"

> Great question. Again, you're right. It's not easy. In fact, it can be a long, challenging road with many incremental steps upward. But rapid progress is also possible. Here's something that may help.
>
> In psychology we call identity beyond the physical world the ego self or the real self or the genuine self. It's a challenge to find that genuine self and be true to it. It takes a great deal of courage to be genuine and authentic and real. We admire those people, but we also hate them. We find them somehow abrasive and offensive because they are absolutely emotionally

honest. If they like something, they like it. If they don't like it, they don't like it and they're not going to pretend they do.

The True Self

A popular argument in the discussion of self is whether genetics or experience plays the dominant role in the development of self-concept. There are strong opinions for both points of view, but others might say that at the end of the day, neither genetics nor socialization really matters. I would say, they both do matter, but it's still not who you are. It's not the true self.

There are many people who have lost parts of their bodies to disease and yet they are still them. Many will tell you they are more of who they genuinely are now than they were when they were physically "whole". Many come to the profound sense that they are more than their physical bodies.

Genuine Self: Embrace Your Uniqueness

Recently I had a conversation with my granddaughter. This is a woman that I believe is absolutely beautiful, talented, extremely intelligent, sensitive, kind and very wise for her age. As you might guess, I think she is perfect.

We were discussing something that she didn't want anyone to know. She was very concerned that if people knew of her heritage that they would not see her for her, or they would judge her because of her more popular and well-known parent. This parent really has not played an active role in her life. However, I believe many of the strengths and gifts she has are because she has had to deal with many hard times and disappointments related to that relationship. She has dealt with this pain with grace and dignity. However, she does feel some shame because she 'is not like the other girls' she knows.

As my beautiful granddaughter and I talked, what kept coming to mind was the phrase, "the truth shall set you free." In reality, we cannot hide who we are. The unconscious attempt to hide only has the impact of alienating us from others and causes the self to fracture – alienating us from our true selves as well. We end up feeling like a fraud, ashamed of who we really are. No one ever consciously plans this, it just happens as we try to navigate this painful journey called life.

Ironically, in the long run it is much less painful to just accept the truth about ourselves. It's like being in the swimming pool with an oversized beach ball that you are trying to keep underwater so no one can see it. You may be able to keep it submerged for a while, but sooner or later it gets free and pops to the surface with a splash for everyone to see. And in reality, all along everyone knew you were hiding something under the water that was keeping you off balance and preoccupied – they just couldn't see it directly.

Angeles Arrien put it nicely in her poem *Show Your Hair*:

My grandmother told me,
'Never hide your green hair –
They can see it anyway.'

The truth is that my granddaughter has nothing to hide. She is complete, whole, and beautiful. She has nothing to apologize for or to be ashamed of. The counsel I gave was," Let everyone see you; they are going to anyway. But learn to stand in the light of your own love and self-acceptance." If she hides what is obvious about her, she loses, and the gifts she has for the world will be lessened.

"Hmm… As I've thought about it, it seems to me that my 'green hair' was related to my perception that I should never out-do my dad," I interjected. "He was a brilliant man, very knowledgeable, competent and respected in his profession, and well-liked by many in the community. I admired him in many ways. But there were a number of areas in which I was much more talented than he was. And yet subconsciously, my belief was that he should always be superior, be right, be the best. It's a very self-limiting place to be, and until now, I didn't even know I was there."

Well, you are taking the first difficult steps toward evaluating and better understanding and loving yourself.

Until we start examining ourselves, our wired domestication shapes our existence, and very few complete the separation cycle that began as an infant and return to connectedness. But the miracle of the brain is that it can be conscious of itself, and conscious of what it thinks. We are the only species on the planet that can be conscious of ourselves. We can think about what we think, and we can choose to believe or disbelieve those thoughts, beliefs, and attitudes.

Folks who never do this are simply bound to repeat the patterns of the past. The mind has the ability to examine the data of the brain and to discern which data is accurate and which is less than accurate. This ability to discern is wisdom.

That consciousness, that ability to evaluate ourselves, is the key to the healing journey. It is fueled by the desire, the commitment, and the courage we give to the journey.

We need not be like the proverbial fish that doesn't know what water is.

I could tell our time was winding down. I was satiated with today's discussion.

So, congratulations, Brad concluded. Your pain and anger with your upbringing – your separation and domestication – brought you to a state of awareness where you are willing to question your domestication and start to move toward the genuine you.

"So, are we going to continue to discuss how to untangle all this domestication, this unconscious wiring of our brains?" I queried.

Absolutely, we'll continue to work through it, Brad replied. But remember, you aren't going to "figure it out" or "think it through." The sensory world that created the pain, that played the major role in your initial wiring or domestication – which for most of us has become overshadowed by the cognitive world – is also the key to healing and wholeness for those with the courage to take the healing journey.

I can't wait for our next meeting," I concluded as I tucked my notebook away. "But for now, my mind needs a rest."

Sounds like a perfect opportunity for some meditation, Brad suggested. "Focus on nothing but your breath."

"Great idea," I said as we parted.

Notes From My Note Pad

Birth = separation, leaving, or moving apart.

The brain records all data. Child's brain records what caregivers think of themselves.

If a parent doesn't love themself, they teach the child not to love itself.

This is an error!! Spell cast on the child.

Highly counterintuitive! The more powerful influence: how much parents loved *themselves*.

Child makes choices considered "mistakes" = actions that threaten the parent's own sense of worth or authority.

Child perceives them as "I *am* a mistake." Not, "I *made* a mistake."

If mistakes become personal (define ourselves by the mistake), we feel shame.

Shame = withdrawing approval of ourselves. Creates deep existential anxiety.

The key: the love of self is the keystone to healing all other relationships

Difficult to find that genuine self and be true to it.

Both genetics and environment matter, but it's not who you

are – not the true self.

Let everyone see your green hair. Be true to your true self.

Pictures From My Sketch Pad

WHOLENESS

⬇

Domestication
"The Spell"

⬇

WOUND

KEY 1
Choose

Choice is a fundamental principle of life, and the starting point for discovering life's gifts.

While the concept of making choices seems fairly straightforward, we often don't see or understand the powerful impact our choices – whether conscious or unconsciously reached – have on our life's situation.

Choosing to begin the journey of discovery requires that we choose to choose, and then keep choosing. That we opt-in 100%. That we choose sometimes-heroic courage to face the dragons that may be lying in wait. That we choose to face the outcomes of our choices that are attached to the other end of the stick we pick up. That we choose to face the painful self-realization, uncomfortable accountability, or unwanted issues that might otherwise be easily avoided. That we choose to see our journey all the way through to the end.

Conscious, purposeful choice ultimately opens the opportunity to discover our greatest personal power and gifts, our deepest relationships, and indescribable personal peace. It's the gateway to our greatest expectations and dreams.

Choice is both simple and profound. It is the first great principle; the first courageous step.

Choice: The First Great Principle

We can't always choose what happens to us, but we are always accountable for what we do with the experience. We are who we choose to be.

Before we jump into today's discussion, I have a little exercise for you, Brad said as we sat down together.

"Sounds good to me," I replied. "I'm up for another day of mental gymnastics."

Okay, here we go, he returned as he began. You have in front of you two bowls of ice cream. One is chocolate, one is vanilla. Which one do you choose?

"Chocolate," I replied

Why chocolate?

"Chocolate has always been my favorite!" I said. "Vanilla is a little bland to me."

That's good, but why do you choose chocolate?

I thought for a minute, then said, "Well, chocolate has a richer flavor than vanilla. It usually isn't as sweet, and it is good for all seasons of the year, whereas vanilla is really only good in the summer."

SECTION 1 : CHOICE: THE FIRST GREAT PRINCIPLE

He said, Great. But why do you choose chocolate?

"I just told you. It's better."

He returned, You told me *about* it, but you didn't tell me *why* you chose it.

I was completely bemused. I couldn't think of any more ways of explaining why I liked chocolate more than vanilla.

Sensing that I might never get it, Brad suggested, You chose chocolate because you *can*. It's that simple. You can choose. It doesn't have to be explained or justified. You just can choose.

"Because I can?" I repeated, almost mechanically.

Yes, because you can. You have ultimate, unfettered choice in life. You don't necessarily have choice over everything that happens to you in life, or what other people choose to do that affects you. But you have complete choice over what you do with what life presents you.

The willingness to choose and take responsibility for the outcomes is the first great principle on the healing journey.

I Am What I Choose, and I Choose What I Am

A good part of my time growing up was spent in the mountains, and I spent a lot of time out among the beauties of this earth. My favorite retreat for thinking, connecting, and just being alone was a remote stand of rare black pine high on a hillside. We called it the Black Timber. I developed a special connection with that place.

Not too long ago, I returned to the Black Timber to once again get away and reconnect. I saddled the horse and began the long, rocky climb to the outcropping near the summit where this magnificent group of trees stood. It was a cold, windy day, but as I approached the grove and dismounted, I felt that warm and inviting embrace just as I had remembered it. I found a quiet spot for contemplation, sat down, took a few deep breaths, closed my eyes, and soaked in the serenity surrounding me.

At that time in my life I was preparing to write a book, and as I sat there I pondered some of the key questions I was exploring. One of them was this: "Who am I?"

Many people when asked this question will say, "I'm a father. I'm a husband. I'm a mother. I'm a wife. I'm a worker. I'm a professional. I'm male. I'm female. I'm transgender." But that's not who we really are.

As I sat there with the wind whistling through the pines, this impression came to me with crystal clarity: "I am who I choose to be." It hit me like it had never hit me before. Who we are is who we choose to be. Everything is a choice. It's as simple as that.

But as I pondered that, I kept asking, "Can it be that simple? Is life really as simple as merely one day choosing who and what we will be?"

The reality is that it both is and isn't that simple. In concept, it's as simple as saying, 'I am who I choose to be, and I choose to be who I am.' But all of our programming says, 'I am my past, I am my body, I am my job, I am my title, I am what happened to me, I am this and that." That programming becomes our reality, how we view our world.

But that view of reality is often simply not true. It's not who we really are. We are our choices. We choose our current level of consciousness, our current view of ourselves and the world, and that view may or may not be aligned with truth and reality. It sounds simple, but for most people, it's a whole new model of reality. New models require us to change, to shift our consciousness. And that's the challenge. That is the healing journey.

The first principle that allows us to take this healing journey is coming to accept that we are fully accountable for creating our life. It is accepting that our life is one we have chosen, either consciously or unconsciously. Either way we are accountable. We may not always choose what happens to us, but we are always accountable for what we do with the experience. We choose our level of consciousness. I think you'll find, as I have, that this fundamental principle is the key to personal empowerment.

I thought for a minute and then interjected, "I think I get the importance of choosing, regardless of what happens to us or how unfairly life may seem to treat us. But aren't there genetic and environmental factors beyond our control that, in a great measure, determine our circumstances and opportunities in life? And doesn't that often overwhelm our ability to choose? It sounds a little simplistic to just say, I choose to be happy."

To conclude that we are just a product of our genes makes us a victim of our genes. Or, if we are just a product of our socialization, then we are victims of our socialization. If we're a product of our psychology, or what people taught us, then we're victims of that. So it doesn't matter what you are a victim to, you're still a victim.

If I say, "I have a predisposition to heart disease," is it certain that I will develop heart disease, or is it just a predisposition? Or if I say, "My family environment was horrific," does that mean that I, too, will have a horrible family life, or is it just a situation? Do I have some sort of opportunity or responsibility in altering those situations, or is it a forgone conclusion?

There is no denying that those things influence us greatly. It's a real part of our lives that we have to deal with. But it's not true that it has made us who we are. Who we are is found at a much deeper and fundamental part of ourselves, at the level of our heart, but we still must deal with the outward influences that shape us so greatly. Who we really are is up to us to rediscover and embrace in the quietness of our souls.

One thing we know about genes at this point is that they can be changed. Environment changes genes. Consciousness changes genes. Our beliefs and thinking about our psychology or our socialization changes them. A whole new field of study called Epigenetics is now making impressive strides in understanding this phenomenon.

But these changes aren't merely a normal, spontaneous part of our existence. Genes change in ways that ultimately benefit us only if we are no longer willing to be a victim of them.

It's one of life's great paradoxes, and ultimately it places the responsibility for how we turn out on ourselves.

SECTION 1 : CHOICE: THE FIRST GREAT PRINCIPLE

My mind was racing. "Another paradox," I thought. "I'm going to have to spend a whole session exploring this paradox thing," Out loud I asked, "What do you mean it's one of life's great paradoxes? I thought you said it was merely a choice. How did it suddenly become a paradox as well?"

> At any level of consciousness, life presents us with a choice of one of two directions, particularly with regard to our pain. We can choose the path of fear, pain avoidance, and resistance, or even denial or over-medication, which leads us to emotional dead ends, or we can choose the path of acceptance, observation, and incorporation, which leads to healing and higher levels of consciousness.
>
> The paradox is that our natural human inclination is to choose the path of fear, and then to justify our decision and its outcomes. But choosing that route obscures our powers of observation that are the key to healing, serenity, and joy.
>
> Let me give you an example of the power of choice.
>
> One night in my cancer group a woman joined us who had recently been diagnosed by her oncologist with Stage 4 cancer.
>
> She didn't want to do chemotherapy. She told her doctor, 'I just want to deal with this myself.' The doctor said, 'That's fine, but we're going to put you on hospice.' To her that meant the doctor was saying, 'You're going to die.' She was very distraught, because she said, 'I want to choose that. I want to choose how I will spend the last part of my life.' But she was distraught because in her world, the doctor was the authority, the doctor was the god, the doctor was giving her the death sentence. And in the scientific world, that's probably pretty

true. She didn't realize that unconsciously she had given her power away to another authority.

As she shared this to the group, I asked, 'Does that sound true to you? What does your true self believe?'

It was fascinating. In the course of about an hour, as I had her just check in with herself, defining what was true for her, she went from being angry, frustrated and upset, to a place where she found peace. You could see it in her countenance as she remembered. All I did was give her an invitation to remember. What I communicated to her was, 'You are in charge of your life.' I didn't actually say those words, but I didn't need to. The situation was presented so she could remember that she was making a choice as to how she dealt with this and the meaning she put on it.

The things we choose to believe are greater and more important than any authority that tells us how we are going to be. In an hour's time this woman felt that healing remembrance of being in charge of her life – of not being a victim. Sure, her body had betrayed her by getting cancer. She was a victim of that diagnosis. She was a victim of the doctor's well-intentioned scientific perspective.

But, the key was, that at the soul level, it wasn't true for her. If all of that had been true for her, she wouldn't have been upset. Her distress was that an idea, a judgement was being presented to her that wasn't true for her. It wasn't congruent with her true self. Genes, experiences, and domestication influence us in measurable ways, but our immeasurable spirit influences them all.

SECTION 1 : CHOICE: THE FIRST GREAT PRINCIPLE

I was enthralled by the power of choice, and the potential I was beginning to glimpse of the impact it could have in my own healing journey. "So choice leads us down one of two paths. Which one are we going to explore first?" I baited Brad, seeing the time was past again.

We'll dive into the path of resistance and victimization next time we meet, he grinned, standing and offering his usual warm embrace. Your assignment is to go and do something you want to do, because you can.

Notes From My Note Pad

Choice is the first great principle of healing

I choose because I can (chocolate!!!) I have complete, unfettered choice in life.

I can't always choose what happens to me, but I have complete choice of what I do with the experience.

"I am who I choose to be": true, and simple in concept. But my programming greatly shapes my view of reality, bends it to not a true, accurate reflection of me. (black timber)

To be a product of my genes or my socialization/environment makes me a victim of them.

Genes can be changed: epigenetics

To be pre-disposed is not to be pre-determined. These things are not who I am.

Who I am is at the soul level – remembered wholeness

Choice is one of life's great paradoxes (find out more about paradox…)

Pictures From My Sketch Pad

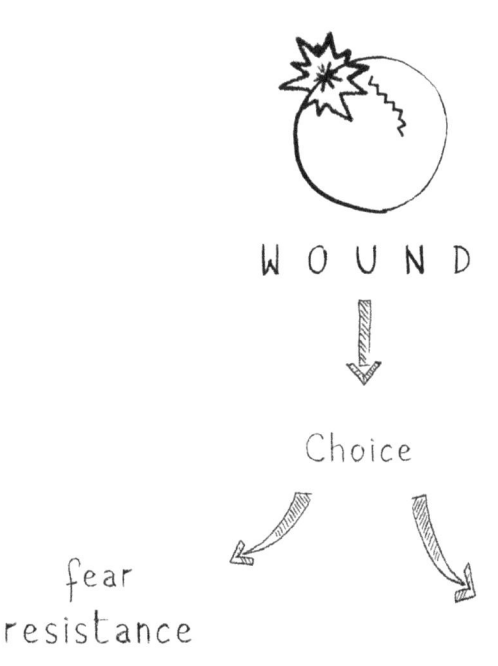

W O U N D

↓

Choice

↙ ↘

fear
resistance
pain

acceptance
observation
true self

KEY 2
Victory Over Victim

There is an old saying that states: "Merely going through life's experiences doesn't teach you anything. The lessons are for those willing to accept the pain of learning."

The reality is that our innate human nature will always take us naturally to the path of lowest pain and least resistance. This wonderful mechanism keeps us safe and stoked with maximum energy to navigate the challenges that threaten our progress or even our very existence. But it also causes our subconscious to construct elaborate ways of reducing the emotional and psychological pain caused by the choices we have made.

In short, our natural tendency is to move to a victim mindset when things don't turn out in a way that meets our expectations. In the short term, this is a much more pain-free, comfortable place to be, rather than admitting that we got ourselves here as a matter of choice. That story becomes hardened with time and repetition, and we find ourselves emotionally stuck, with no clear idea of why or how to get out.

Key 2 is to learn to recognize our "stuck" stories, and understand how we can begin to free ourselves to move beyond a victim mindset.

Victory Over Victim: Dead Ends

Following our natural instincts to avoid pain will leave us locked in false stories, caustic depression, or even addiction.

I had fun that week trying on the idea of choosing because I can. I started adding "because I can" to every decision I made, just to enjoy the novelty of it. "I go to work at 8:00 am- because I can," or, "I'm wearing my striped shirt today- because I can."

But as time went on and I thought it through more deeply, I recognized that many of my more important choices- such as those that impact my marriage, key relationships, and direction in life- were not completely based on my core desires and needs, but were often overly influenced by trying to accommodate someone else's needs, wants, and opinions.

I thought of this as I came to Brad's office. Brad greeted me at the door and ushered me into the room.

So, how did choosing go this week? he asked.

"I really got into the 'because I can' thing," I replied. "But I recognized how deeply influenced I am by others' wants and desires that aren't congruent with being true to me. Most interesting was the realization that is several cases, my perception of another person's wants and needs wasn't even accurate. So I was choosing based

SECTION 1 : VICTORY OVER VICTIM: DEAD ENDS

on something that wasn't true for me *or* the person I thought I was accommodating."

I appreciate your work, Brad replied. If you're committed and open, many revealing insights can come to you.

I was always a little thrown off by Brad's unique way of responding. But interesting as it was, I was anxious to pick up our conversation where we had left off the previous week.

"I'm ready to explore this idea of choice as related to victimization and story stuck-ness you mentioned last time," I suggested.

Okay, let's dive in, Brad replied.

Once we are aware of our wounds, we are faced with a choice. Wounding doesn't automatically result in understanding. Rather, it presents us a choice to either seek deeper understanding, or to follow our natural human instinct to avoid, deny, medicate, or otherwise eliminate the pain.

Ultimately, our natural instinct to avoid pain is rooted in fear: fear that this pain is a reflection on us, and says that we are somehow not loved, not enough, we don't measure up, that we are not exceptional, that no one cares. It is the fear that there is no purpose in this pain and this experience, and therefore no purpose or fairness in life.

To salve the wound, we create a story that justifies our position and makes us feel better about ourselves. The problem with this story is that it is rarely based in reality, and it typically includes blaming someone or something else for our situation rather than owning it ourselves.

The Victim Paradox

The conscious journey is to recognize and resolve the dichotomy or paradox of being victimized, but choosing to not be a victim. It is to recognize that though the world can kill us, maim us, strike us with disease, or raise us in an environment of abuse, those things are still *not who we are*. Yes, we are in the world; we are still subject to genes, environment, and other people's consciousness, but we still have the choice to behave in a way that will help our soul and enlighten our consciousness.

To paraphrase, it's being in the world, but not being a victim of the world.

I began thinking of people I knew who might fit the profile of victim. One man came to mind whom I had met 10 years earlier. "Is this what you mean by being a victim, being 'of the world?'" I asked.

"This friend is a very capable man, highly educated, articulate, driven, and creative. He runs his own business, has spoken all over the world, and has a reasonably comfortable life. As we were getting to know one another, I asked him about his background and his business. He told me a little about what he currently does, but then recounted in some detail the events of a business situation years earlier where he had done a significant amount of work on a product with a partner. He had done most of the work, and was preparing it for sale, for which he had a great deal of experience.

"At the last minute, the partner decided to bring in another person to launch it, and basically cut him out of the deal, including the royalties and residuals he would have been entitled to. He emphasized the devious nature of this partner, how he went on to make a fortune, and how he would have been nothing without the work my friend had done early on for him.

"There was significant bitterness and contempt in his voice, even after all the years that had passed.

"I noticed a couple of interesting things as our friendship developed. First was how frequently he repeated this experience. It wasn't always a complete recounting of the incidents, but often he would rehearse portions of the story, or make snide remarks about situations that resembled his experience – obvious references to his wounding and anger over these incidents.

"Over time I also came to realize that I was hearing a filtered version of the story. At various times in the numerous recountings, I would find myself thinking, 'You know, if I were your partner, I may have done the same thing. This version of the story sounds a little skewed.' I realized that over time he had assigned motive to many of the interactions, and his perception of the truth was tainted by his view and memory of the situation.

"So here he was, 25 years later, angry and hurt and bitter. He just couldn't let it go. He couldn't stop telling the story."

> Brad nodded. That was obviously a highly traumatic experience for him. It's likely his partner actually did many of those painful things to him. Your friend was victimized in ways that to one extent or another were outside of his control.
>
> He took that experience of being victimized, and chose to remain the victim. In order to avoid dealing with the pain, he crafted a story that justified his hurt and offense. He made it about someone or something else, not about him.

Then he constantly re-told the story to salve his wounds and reassure himself that he's right, they're wrong, and he's not responsible for his current situation. That is exactly how victims think.

If life is pain, it is also victimization. Just as every human will be wounded and experience pain of varying types and degrees, every human will be victimized as well.

As you observed with your friend, victims are either angry or depressed, and often both. They have chosen one of the dead ends to healing and awareness. It's what we call being stuck in the story.

"Stuck in the story", I mused. "That a great description. Now that I think about it, while I like him and value our friendship, being around him can really wear on me. The cynicism and anger are draining."

Victims often find it hard to form close relationships, because they live in stories that are based on their own ego-based version of reality rather than truth, acceptance and love. If you observe carefully and listen to language, you can spot the victim-ness in people.

I started a list as Brad ticked off the general characteristics:

Blameful
It's always someone or something else's fault

Vengeful
They're often obsessed with evening the score

SECTION 1 : VICTORY OVER VICTIM: DEAD ENDS

Vindictive
They are aggressive crusaders to prove they are right

Inflexible
"That's my story and I'm sticking to it."

Dismissing
Deny any hurt or pain; use intimidation to protect story

Discontent
They complain about things they deal with in everyday life, and spend countless hours finding fault with others who are trying and falling short.

Arrogant
They tend to overinflate their importance or how spotless and innocent they are with regard to the players in the story.

> As you've probably observed, most people don't live a life of a total victim. But there are aspects of life that we choose to resist, and thus live to some extent as victims.

I looked at the outline and asked, "You mentioned victims have chosen one of the infamous "dead ends" to healing and consciousness. Are there other dead ends?"

> Another dead-end mind set is bitterness. I simply call them bitter. These are people who have chosen to protect their story by filling their lives with bitterness and cynicism. Much like their victim counterparts, bitters are stuck in the story of their own building, reinforced by the walls of bitterness they build around it. Here's how to spot them:

Cynical
They are often highly cynical and sarcastic in their approach to life and relationships

Angry
They become agitated, particularly around topics they are being cynical about. The anger and poison are often way out of proportion with the circumstance.

Critical
They are quick to point out flaws and errors, particularly among those whom they believe "should know better" or "should set the example."

Divisive
They love to be controversial, and enjoy starting a disagreement or fight and then stepping back and watching the fireworks.

Depressed
Because they are bitter and angry, they are also often depressed.

Ultra-competitive
They love to one-up or beat someone else, and gloat over victory and complain at defeat

Have to be right
These people are nearly obsessed with being right and winning. They don't take kindly to others disagreeing with them or proving them wrong.

SECTION 1 : VICTORY OVER VICTIM: DEAD ENDS

Arrogance

Along with competitiveness and being right, they tend to overestimate their brilliance, capability and prowess.

A more severe dead end is addiction, because it can be so devastating to many aspects of life.

Addiction

Addictions are attempted solutions to problems not acknowledged. The purpose of all addictive behaviors is an attempt to nurture and comfort the inner self. Addictions create a false connection with self that reduces the anxiety of being separate, or not loving yourself. It's the side effects of this false connection that create so many problems for the person who choses this solution to a problem.

An addiction gives the illusion of being connected, which is temporarily comforting. But the illusion is what creates the deep pain – because it ultimately makes us feel more separate from ourselves and from those whom we need love from. Addictive behaviors give us the illusion of having a spiritual experience but while true spiritual experiences leave us feeling more, the illusion of a spiritual experience leaves us feeling less.

Addiction is something we do, not something we are. If we believe we are an addict, and we say, "I'm an addict," then we are one, and it becomes manifest in our behavior. It becomes something that defines us.

There are times when these powerful psychological experiences cannot be differentiated from the real spiritual transformation and must be reality-tested with someone who is trusted and safe. The fruits born of a genuine, authentic spiritual experience hurt neither the person who has it nor the people loved by that person.

Brad stopped and I finished my note. "So resistance to pain leads us to the dead ends of victim, bitter and addict," I recapped. "We get on that path through our own fear of not being enough or not measuring up."

That's right, said Brad. The irony is that the more you resist the pain, the more it grows. Pushing against it, fighting it, denying it, or avoiding it, including by over-medicating it, only makes it worse. It doesn't go away, it actually intensifies.

As you dig in in this way, you actually become a slave to the wound, rather than being freed by the lessons it contains. Becoming victim to the wound, you give away your personal power and become defined by it. For example, I hear people say, "I'm a rape victim, I'm divorced, we were bankrupt, etc." They've built a story around their pain, chosen the victim road, and now consciously or unconsciously define themselves by the pain of the wound. In essence, they now own the very thing they are trying to avoid.

To add to the challenge, we reinforce victim, bitter and addict by throwing in codependence. It's like a flywheel that keeps us continually spinning around in our chosen dead-end story.

"What do you mean by codependence?" I asked.

Volumes have been written and studied on the subject, but quite simply, codependence is looking outside ourselves for validation and happiness, rather than finding it intrinsically in our own genuine selves.

I work with clients all the time who say things like, "Yeah, our marriage is bad, but if she would just do this and this, I could really be happy with her." It's wanting people to be the way you want them to be in order for you to be happy. When you are a victim, bitter, or an addict, you are looking for others to validate your story, not to question your motives or expose the possible inaccuracies in your positions.

In codependence, you are highly dependent on others' opinions and define your worth by what they say about you. Because of that, you are also easily offended by opinions that don't fit your story and perceptions. With the offense usually comes justification or blame, meaning you make it about them, or about you.

I knew our time was short, but my insides were starting to churn. I was deep in thought about Brad's comments on the victim dead end.

You look troubled.

Brad's voice broke in to the depth of my contemplation. Where are you?

I was silent for a moment, collecting my thoughts and emotions. "I was thinking about victim, and suddenly had this sick, gripping feeling that the victim story sounds frighteningly familiar. It's a terrifying thought. I just realized that when you asked me, 'How's that working for you?' a while back, you were actually asking, 'How's that victim story playing out for you?' It's like a bolt of lightning that's both brilliantly illuminating and illuminatingly awful."

> I could see early on you were pretty stuck in your story, Brad replied. Along with the anger and depression, it was pretty clear you were thoroughly stuck in a victim dead end. When we raise our level of consciousness, as you are currently, it's both exhilarating and devastating. We feel free of the fetters of error that have bound us for so long. But at the same time, we have the awful recognition of the pain and disruption we have caused in our own lives and in the lives of those we've interacted with.

"Yeah, that's the dichotomy I'm living right now, recognizing how much of a victim I've been for so many years," I returned. "But I'm still conflicted. How do I reconcile what I now understand with what it seems happened to me that was beyond my control?"

> You are experiencing one of life's deepest and most important paradoxes, Brad replied.

"Okay, that's it. You keep mentioning paradoxes," I said. "Are you ever going to tell me what it means?"

> Hmmm…The dilemma is, we have a very important topic, and no time to discuss it, Brad replied with a mischievous smile.

"It seems like we never have enough time. Is there a psychological name for that dilemma?" I asked.

> You might call it a paradox paradox, Brad replied.

"Perfect," I replied. "A paradox paradox. It will take a miracle to

SECTION 1 : VICTORY OVER VICTIM: DEAD ENDS

unwind that one!"

Well, you've experienced a bit of a miracle here today already, Brad returned. No reason to expect anything less next time around."

I folded my pad, gave Brad my customary man hug, and walked to the car deep in thought.

Notes From My Note Pad

Pain resistance is based on fear: that we're not loved, don't measure up, not exceptional

To reduce pain of the wound, we create a story that justifies our position, a story that justifies our position, usually not based in reality.

Often blame someone/something else vs. owing it

Leads to Dead Ends

We become a slave to the wound

Defined by it; give it our power; own it

The Dead Ends

Victim

We are all victimized – often have little control over what

happens to us

What we do with it – becoming victim – is a choice

What happened to us is NOT who or what we are

"In the world, but not of the world"

Bitter

Protect your story with bitterness and cynicism.

Stuck in own stories

Addict

Purpose of addiction: attempt to nurture and comfort the inner self.

Gives illusion of being connected, but the illusion creates deep pain –makes us feel more separate from ourselves, loved ones.

Codependence Fly Wheel – keeps you stuck

Want people to be the way you want them to be in order for you to be happy

Define your worth by others' opinions

Easily offended – make it about them or you

PARADOX AGAIN! This time, a paradox paradox

Quotes From My Quote Book

Pain resisted intensifies. Becomes a story. Leads to victim. Stuck in the story.

"If life is pain, it is also victimization. Just as every human will be wounded and experience pain of varying types and degrees, every human will be victimized as well. It's the meaning we put on that victimization that determines whether we become the victim."

— C. Bradford Chappell

Pictures From My Sketch Pad

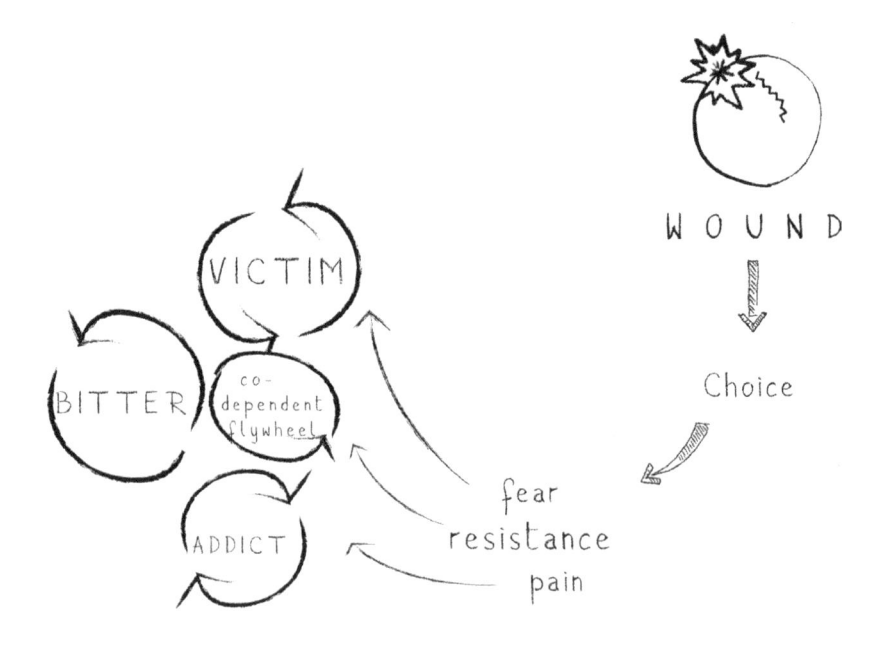

SECTION 2
The Pool We Swim In: Paradox and the Linear Model

SECTION 2: THE POOL WE SWIM IN: PARADOX AND THE LINEAR MODEL

The better we understand our perceptual swimming pool, the better equipped we are to navigate through it. Two additional foundational concepts help clarify our understanding, and provide better line-of-sight for swimming to clearer waters.

Paradox is the second great principle (choice is #1) we must come to grips with in our journey of discovery, and is another influence largely unnoticed, misunderstood and ignored along the path. The first chapter in this section will help clarify the concept of paradox and how it applies to nearly everything we experience in life. We'll also explore a disarmingly simple method of making paradox an ally rather than a stumbling block along the way.

For many people, the journey of discovery is also impeded by resistance to considering all inputs available for increased understanding. Many of these inputs lie along what is known as the non-linear, or sensory dimension of our perceived reality. The second chapter of this section contrasts the linear and non-linear dimensions, and introduces a model that presents the powerful insights available through the latter.

We'll then move on to understand the next three keys of discovering the gift in the wound. Key 3, The Pain Portal, introduces the counter-intuitive concept of pain and the pain paradox – the pivotal turning point in many healing journeys. In three chapters we'll better understand pain and the purpose of pain, the pain paradox, and the accelerating power of bringing militant-level commitment to our discovery efforts.

Key 4 is called "I Love Me." This key illustrates the crucial importance and illuminating power of love of self and others that comes through understanding and implementing gratitude and forgiveness, with one chapter devoted to each principle.

The last key, Key 5 – known as "Effortless Acceptance" – discusses the surprisingly simple capstone step of the journey in a chapter that describes how acceptance can flow to us through intuition, not our own effort.

In the final chapter of this section we'll explore how we can enhance and accelerate effortless acceptance by creating the space for ultimate healing to take place.

Understanding the five keys as well as the environment we operate in can provide a clear, empowering path to discovering the gift in the wound.

Paradox: The Second Great Principle

Seemingly juxtaposed ideas can be reconciled by viewing them in terms of 'and' rather than 'either/or,' giving us the space to move forward.

The next time I sat down with Brad, we briefly reviewed some of the key concepts we had discussed: the power of choice, and choosing not just what you will be in life, but choosing what to do with the challenges, wounds, and pain that come to you. We spoke of how we have the choice to be the victim and build an elaborate story around those experiences, or to view them as potential opportunities for greater consciousness, understanding and wisdom.

Remember, choice is the first great principle of the healing journey, he concluded. Today, we're going to move on to the next principle.

"That's great, but I don't want to go any further until I figure out this paradox thing," I interjected.

Well, it just so happens that paradox is the second great principle. So today's your lucky day.

"Finally!" I replied. "I hope this is worth the wait," I quipped.

It's true, I did delay our discussion, Brad began. But the angst you experienced was your own choice in dealing with it, he winked. I realized I had just failed a pop quiz on last week's discussion. At any rate, I think you'll enjoy this idea, he quickly added.

"Okay, I'm willing to move into the pain," I shot back, arming myself with pen and pad.

The second great principle of the healing journey is coming to understand paradox and how it can be useful in dealing with life's painful experiences.

Our lives are filled with paradox. We commonly call it comic irony, bitter irony, or poetic justice, depending on who is on which end of the outcomes. For many, it only makes for intriguing reading and engaging plots, while others find it deeply troubling and unfair, using it as fuel for their fires of victimization. Either way, paradox is a real and integral part of our existence on this planet. And not only does it touch every human life, but paradox is at the heart of virtually every experience essential to human healing. If we don't resolve these apparent contradictions, we don't heal.

At its core, a paradox is an idea that seems self-contradictory or absurd, but in reality expresses a possible truth. Resolving it involves the ability to hold two seemingly opposing ideas in our minds and find meaning in them.

Unresolved paradoxes leave us feeling conflicted and unfulfilled. There is no harmony or balance, and healing is impossible. Our pain becomes purposeless. On the other hand, resolved paradox allows us to create a connection that brings love into our lives and gives meaning to contradictory or unwanted experiences.

SECTION 2 : PARADOX: THE SECOND GREAT PRINCIPLE

"Can you give me a couple of examples of paradox in people's lives?" I asked.

Sure. Think about this: Many people who have gone through very difficult experiences will say that it was the best time of their lives. Many who have experienced the horrors of war say it was a time when they felt most alive. Most would never want to go through the terrible or horrible times again, but within that experience there were things that they were so grateful for, things they say they would never trade for any amount of money.

Here's another example: In our society today, particularly in the West among younger people, there is talk and a desire to be connected with many other humans on the earth. If we're connected, that essentially makes you and me the same in that we are made up of exactly the same molecules and atoms and all have the same basic needs.

But, having said that, we all have absolutely unique needs. We are also separate. There is a boundary between us. My body ends at my skin; yours starts at the beginning of your skin. So we're very separate.

If I look at this purely from an ego standpoint, our separateness somehow means we're different and that I'm better and superior or worse and inferior than you. Which means we can't be the same, we can't be connected. It's a contradiction that can't be resolved from this level of consciousness.

If I'm going to resolve this paradox, a higher level of consciousness allows me to love that separateness and at the same time see that we are both connected by something beyond myself- a brotherhood, a community, or mere humanity. We're separate, but we have an emotional connection in how we see the world. And as I help you meet your needs, I am also meeting my own. As I serve you I am serving myself.

When we are able to move beyond ego differences, we will see that we are more the same than we are different, that the stuff that really matters is the stuff that we all want and need. This is the stuff of the heart that is most precious. And that is the inherent beauty of the paradox.

"Hmmmm…" I said as I jotted a few notes. "So this higher level of consciousness you speak of is the ability to hold these two conflicting ideas in your mind at the same time and resolve them. That sounds theoretically possible, but not something that comes naturally to any of us. How do I just raise my consciousness?"

Here's the key, Brad continued, and it's actually a lot simpler than it sounds.

"And," vs "Either/Or"

Unresolved paradox is always viewed as 'either/or'- it's either this way or that way, and it can't be both. In our minds we are considering two seemingly opposing and irreconcilable ideas.

The key to resolving a paradox is to shift our thinking from 'either/or' to 'and.' This paradigm shift allows us to hold two seemingly opposing ideas in harmony with each other.

Jesus Christ gave a great example of this kind of resolution when he answered the question, "Who shall we worship, God or Caesar?"

SECTION 2 : PARADOX: THE SECOND GREAT PRINCIPLE

He called for a coin, and asked, "Whose inscription is this on the coin?

"Caesar's," was the reply.

"Then render unto Caesar that which is Caesar's and unto God that which is God's."[2]

He resolved the paradox. The Jews viewed the question as 'either/or' – worship God or Caesar. He shifted their consciousness to a higher level. He invited them to view a problem from a different paradigm, and rather than think 'either/or', he shifted to an 'and' paradigm which resolved the problem. As soon as you make it 'and', the ideas are connected and harmonized.

That's the key. Resolving paradox always comes in the form of finding the 'and.' But therein lies the challenge. Our egos, being exclusionary, competitive and protective, always naturally move toward 'either/or."

"Let me see if I get this," I said. "I'm grappling with this paradox of my business partner – or more accurately, my former business partner. This guy was a dream to work with until we had a final product ready for marketing, at which point he took the intellectual property, cut me out of the deal, and marketed it himself. Attorneys didn't give me much hope of recovering anything, so I finally gave up the fight.

It's terribly ironic to me that even though many of the best features of this product were my ideas, I'm the one who is now suffering financially, and he's skating free to the adoration of all who buy from him. But despite my frustration towards him, my background teaches me that I'm supposed to forgive this guy who doesn't deserve to be forgiven. How's that for a paradox?"

So, he's the bad guy and doesn't deserve the rewards or to be forgiven, but because of your beliefs, and against your desire and common sense, you feel that you should forgive him. Is that right? Brad summarized.

"Yeah, that's about it," I replied.

Well, there's the either/or of the paradox. And from your current viewpoint, it is un-resolvable. It is one or the other.

"Okay, and…" I probed.

Your job is to find the 'and' in the equation, how it can be both at the same time, and that comes from viewing it from a higher level of consciousness or experience or insight. Maybe there's something in the experience you aren't seeing, or haven't considered. Maybe there's an aspect of pay or value that you haven't thought about. Maybe there's an angle of success, for him or for you, that you haven't explored. There are always many facets to a paradox.

Honestly, I don't know what the answer is. Only you can discover it. We won't resolve it today, but if you are willing, I promise you it will come to you. You will find your 'and.'

So my friend, I invite you to move beyond your current perceptions, quiet your mind, and listen to your heart. Life has presented you with a rare gift to raise your level of consciousness, to practice getting out of victimhood, and to find the deeper meaning of your experiences.

SECTION 2 : PARADOX: THE SECOND GREAT PRINCIPLE

"Sometimes it seems it would be a lot easier if you just gave me the answers," I said as I jotted a few more notes. "It'll be hard enough to figure out my 'and,' but there are other intriguing concepts you talk about. Like what does 'linearity' mean? Or 'level of consciousness?' When can we talk about those?"

It will come in time, Brad replied as he stood – signaling that our session was ending. Your answer will come. Don't force it. Let it come to you. And the next time we meet, I'll try to shed a little light on some of those concepts that maybe aren't as clear to you.

"Okay, but this is totally uncharted territory," I replied. We shook hands and I set off on my quest to resolve my paradox.

Notes From My Note Pad

Paradox is the unresolved juxtaposition of two seemingly conflicting ideas – always expressed as "either/or

Touches us all – at the heart of all healing experiences.

If we don't resolve paradoxes, we don't heal.

The key to resolving paradox: shift from "either/or" to finding "and" – shift our consciousness

A paradox can't be resolved at the same level of consciousness that created it

Requires us to think outside our current framework and

consider other possibilities

Listen to your heart, quiet your mind, find insight, consciousness and love = You will find the "and"!

Brad's commitment: talk about "linear" and levels of consciousness!

Two Views of Reality: Linear and Non-Linear

Reality can be split into two points of view: time and perspective. If we enlarge our perspective, then we experience healing in time.

I was anxious to follow up on our previous discussion when we got together for our next meeting.

So, how was your week? he began as we sat down. Did you resolve your paradox?

"Actually, I found an 'and' in my dilemma" I replied. "I think I better understand paradox, and want to bounce my ideas off you," I said.

"*And* – exactly," he shot back.

But, before we get into that, I want to make sure we have time to discuss the concepts we postponed last time. A number of times you've referred to the term 'linear: linear thinking, linear medicine, a linear approach. Exactly what do you mean by linear?"

It has reference to the two dimensions of reality we live in, Brad began. I was excited to finally understand this term he used so frequently.

Two Dimensions of Reality

To navigate life successfully we must be aware of the two dimensions that make up our reality. They are so much a part of our reality that most of us never stop to even consider their existence or how they interact with each other on a continuous basis. They are much like our breath: so common we never think about it until we start to lose it. For most people, these dimensions remain an unconscious part of their existence.

There are two dimensions or directions of thought: vertical and horizontal. By making these dimensions a part of our conscious thought, it will help us to better apply the principle of choice by allowing us to consciously choose the meaning we give to our experience. To do this, though, we must understand what each dimension represents.

Brad got up, opened a white board hidden behind a cabinet on the wall, and picked up a green marker pen. He drew a horizontal line across the middle of the board.

The Horizontal Dimension: Linearity

The horizontal dimension is the dimension of linearity, or linear existence. It is defined by time and is perceived as past, present, and future. This is the dimension of of opposites: birth and death, right and wrong, good and bad. There is always a beginning and an end. In this dimension existence is either/or and is always temporary.

Linearity exists for every material entity that comes on the planet, and it always goes in one direction. The seed becomes the plant. The lamb becomes the sheep. The child becomes the adult. The plant never goes back to being the seed from which it sprang. The lamb never goes back to its wooly innocence. The child never returns to its limited abilities and helplessness. The linear dimension defines most things in the material world.

The world of science lives on this dimension. Things are observed, measured, quantified, and analyze, to see if what we think we are seeing is really what we are seeing. The big bang is a linear model. There was a beginning and there is going to be an end. Our wonderful medical science was developed through the linear, scientific method.

Throughout our domestication in early life, we are taught to think linearly. This is not a conscious process any more than learning a first language is a conscious process. We simply learn it because we are exposed to it and the brain records it.

For example, our educational models are based on linearity. We build on previous information that has been 'downloaded' into the brain. We are not even aware that this information is being recorded. In our formal education process, we go from kindergarten to grade school to junior high to high school to college. We go through a sequence with a starting point and an end point. If something is not learned in this process, for example, not learning to read, it impacts us the rest of our lives.

Linearity is very much a function of our Western paradigm. Without ever intending to, our domestication wires us to think linearly. It is impossible to not be aware of the cause-and-effect relationships that govern our lives. This level of thinking is essential to our very survival as a species.

The Vertical Dimension – Levels of Consciousness

Brad picked up the pen and drew a simple vertical line intersecting the linear line in the center.

> The vertical dimension is the dimension of consciousness or awareness. It is the meaning we put on the experiences we have in the linear dimension. We are, in fact, meaning-making organisms and, either consciously or not, we're putting meaning on all of our life experiences. While we may not always choose what happens to us, if we are willing, we can always choose what meaning we put on an event. It is, however, something we must choose, and it often goes against our natural, instinctual tendencies.
>
> We refer to this meaning we assign as consciousness, or levels of consciousness. There is no negative consciousness, no negative awareness – just lower or higher awareness. Higher consciousness is always preferable to a lower level of consciousness.
>
> There are infinite levels of consciousness, each with its own set of attitudes and beliefs. Higher consciousness can be aware of lower consciousness, but lower cannot know or understand higher consciousness.
>
> While different, each level of consciousness is still perfect. Whatever level of awareness you have is a perfect level of awareness – meaning that it is what it is, and the person is operating exactly as their level of consciousness dictates. Perfect doesn't mean it's complete. For example, if a person shows an act of kindness, it is a perfect act of kindness for their level of awareness. If a person shows an act of hatred, it is a perfect act of hatred. Acts of kindness are preferable to acts of hatred,

but often it is the acts of hatred that motivate us to do better as individuals and as a society.

The meaning we assign to an experience – our level of consciousness at the time – can change as consciousness evolves. For example, in the cancer group, many enter thinking that their life is a catastrophe, but leave realizing that having cancer, while very difficult, has made the sanctity of life so much more poignant and led them to vistas of understanding that they otherwise never would have had.

The vertical dimension is also the dimension of now. Nothing is ever happening in the past or in the future. Whatever level of consciousness you have, you have it now. Whatever you are thinking, you are thinking it now. Events and things on this dimension happen only in the present. It means choosing in this moment how we are going to view the present moment.

As opposed to the linear dimension, this is the sensory dimension. It can't be measured, quantified, thought, or figured out. It can only be sensed. Many people recognize this dimension even though they can't measure or really explain it. We call it intuition or hunches or intuitive feelings. It's a sensory, non-linear experience and it comes through a process we call inspiration.

Brad drew a circle at the bottom of the vertical dimension line.

The psychological meaning we put on experiences is we call consciousness. In this dimension, consciousness is determined in a large part by the particular cultural environment we are born into. Linear consciousness comes naturally to all of us, because of our domestication/socialization. Because it is linear-based, it is generally a fairly low level of consciousness.

I was sketching my own version of the model in my notebook, inserting some of the details Brad was referring to.

"So the linear dimension is the dimension of duality, of past, present, and future, and of measurement. Would judgement be a linear function, since it's a measurement?" I asked.

Absolutely.

"Okay, I think I'm getting it. But an example would really help," I replied.

Well, let's go back to your paradox – that's a perfect example. Last time we met, you described a paradox in linear terms. Your partner stabbed you in the back, stole your ideas and work, and enriched himself at your expense. I'm guessing you could even tell me approximately what that has cost you in money, time, and career advancement, right?

"Yes, I've gone through those calculations a hundred times."

"Actually, the experience with your partner just described which created this paradox is an incident in the past, a form of pain, that we could put on the linear dimension here in the past," Brad continued, drawing a circle on the linear line to the left of the vertical dimension. "The meaning you put on that experience is your level of consciousness, which we'll plot down here," he said, drawing a circle in the lower portion of the vertical dimension line. "From your current level of consciousness you see this as the paradox of either he's the bad guy and doesn't deserve to be forgiven, or you deserve recognition and payment for your ideas – and you see no hope for resolution."

SECTION 2 : TWO VIEWS OF REALITY: LINEAR AND NON-LINEAR

"Yes that was how I was viewing it, until you challenged me to find the 'and.' Last week I happened across a great insight in a little book you gave me called *The Four Agreements*. In it he says, 'We forgive others not because they deserve to be forgiven, but because we love ourselves so much that we don't want to keep paying for the injustice.'

That insight hit me right between the eyes, and I realized I had discovered my 'and': What my partner did wasn't right, AND I'm stopping my progress by continually rehearsing and holding onto that injustice. In other words, AND I am willing to let go of it, not because he deserves it, but because I love myself enough that I don't want to keep paying for what happened.

> "There you go. You've just raised your level of consciousness, the meaning you put on that incident, and resolved the paradox," Brad replied. He drew a circle on the vertical line above the original consciousness circle, indicating a higher level of consciousness.

"Interestingly, as we're talking and thinking about it, I just realized that while what he did was totally wrong, the more I think about his approach and our relationship, I realize that his actions were based on a deep fear. I'm not sure what the root of that fear is, but I now understand that from that mindset, he did the best he could – which was to take advantage of me to protect himself. That's all he was capable of," I mused. "Crazy as it sounds, I actually sincerely feel sorry for the guy."

> Brad drew another circle above the previous one. Your consciousness is continuing to expand, he said. The meaning you just put on that incident is radically different than the one you originally described to me. And most importantly, the change

in your demeanor is obvious. Whereas before you were agitated, angry, confused and frustrated, now I sense peace, calm and compassion.

"Amazing," I said. "I never thought I'd get to this point on something so devastating in my life. And it happened relatively quickly."

It's always effortless when we connect with our inner truth. You sensed it. You didn't figure it out, think it through, or apply a formula. The insight came to you in the present.

Brad put down the pen and returned to his chair. This model can help put in perspective many of the difficult challenges we face in life.

"Are we done already?" I queried, glancing at the clock. "I can't believe how the time flew."

It's a great illustration of working on the non-linear dimension. Since it's not time-bound, when we're dealing with consciousness matters, it can seem to our minds like time has slowed or even stopped. But there are a few minutes left.

The Healing Path

"Since we're drawing on the board and we still have some time, I've got a picture of my own to show you," I offered.

Great. I'd love to see it.

I went to the white board and began to draw.

"Here's where it all started – with wholeness," I said, drawing a circle at the top of the board. "At some point we experience a wound, which causes pain."

"When we experience the pain, we have a choice. We can go into fear and follow our natural inclination and resist or avoid the pain – putting us on the path to the dead ends."

"The circles represent the stories, and being stuck in an endless loop of the story around the pain."

"This is the flywheel of codependence which helps keep the stories spinning and keep us stuck."

That's very good, Brad mused as he studied the diagram. It sums up the path and interactions quite well.

"Here's the interesting part that just came to me recently," I continued. "This is the 'stuck-in-the-story cycle. It goes like this:

Ouch! – Grrrr – Bla-bla-bla

What do you mean, Ouch, Grrrr, Bla-bla-bla? Brad asked.

I wrote the three words on the board. "It's the loop of being stuck in the story. Ouch! is the pain we are resisting that starts the cycle. It could be remembering a wounding experience, regretting a past action, reliving a victimizing trauma, realizing yet again a major mistake or botched relationship, or a thousand other wounds. It's the pain from whatever wound we are dealing with at the time. Because we resist it, we get into a 'Grrrr' mode of setting our jaw, baring our claws, pushing back, and resisting. This soon leads to the 'Grrrr' of anger, frustration, envy, revenge, and depression." I wrote some of these terms below this second step.

"Because we are hurt and angry and depressed, we feel we have to justify our position, so we cook up a story to salve our wounds. This concocted tale is full of justification, blame, and accusations that we endlessly bla-bla-bla to anyone who will listen." I wrote some of this below the third word.

"Because this is a repeating cycle, these are actually in a circular pattern, like this," I said, putting the three words in a circle connected by curving arrows. "We feel the pain, we resist and get angry or depressed, we tell our story again – and then it happens all over again next time we think of that particular wound."

"So, it's the Ouch! Grrrr… Bla-bla-bla cycle," I said, writing the words around the three dead end circles, "that keep us stuck in Victim, Bitter and Addict."

    That's really very good, Brad replied. I'm glad to see my explanations mapped out with such simple clarity for you. It's easy to get lost in the process when life gets messy – which it always does.

"The time always goes too fast. I'm just getting warmed up," I said as we shook hands.

    That sounds like a 'Grrrr', Brad replied. You'd better get out of here before you start into the 'Bla-bla-bla.'

"Good point," I said, and hurried toward the door.

SECTION 2 : TWO VIEWS OF REALITY: LINEAR AND NON-LINEAR

Notes From My Note Pad

Two Dimension of Reality

Horizontal dimension: the dimension of linearity

Dimension of time; events happen in the past, present and future

Duality, opposites: beginning/end, birth/death, right/wrong, good/bad, either/or

Always temporary

Dimension of science: observed, measured

Vertical dimension: the dimension of consciousness or awareness

The meaning we put on the experiences of the linear dimension

We don't always choose what happens to us (linear dimension); but, if willing, can always choose what meaning we put on any event

Must choose! Often goes against natural instincts

The dimension of NOW.

Events on this dimension are always finite = they happen only in the present.

No negative consciousness, only higher or lower consciousness;

Higher is always preferred.

Higher can know lower, but not vice-versa

The *sensory* dimension. Can't be measured, quantified.

Can't be thought, figured out. Can only be *sensed*.

We call it intuition, hunches, things manifested to us, inspiration.

Many scientists refuse to consider the vertical dimension;

Quotes From My Quote Book

Pain resisted intensifies. Becomes a story. Leads to victim.

Stuck in the story.

bla-bla-bla

SECTION 2 : TWO VIEWS OF REALITY : LINEAR AND NON-LINEAR

Pictures From My Sketch Pad

LINEAR DIMENSION

Birth / Beginning
Duality / Time / Space / Measurable
Death / End

Good / Past
Laws of Physics
Bad / Future

NON-LINEAR DIMENSION

Can't be Measured

Can't be Thought

Can Only be Sensed

Dimensions of Consciousness

The Present / Now

Levels of Consciousness

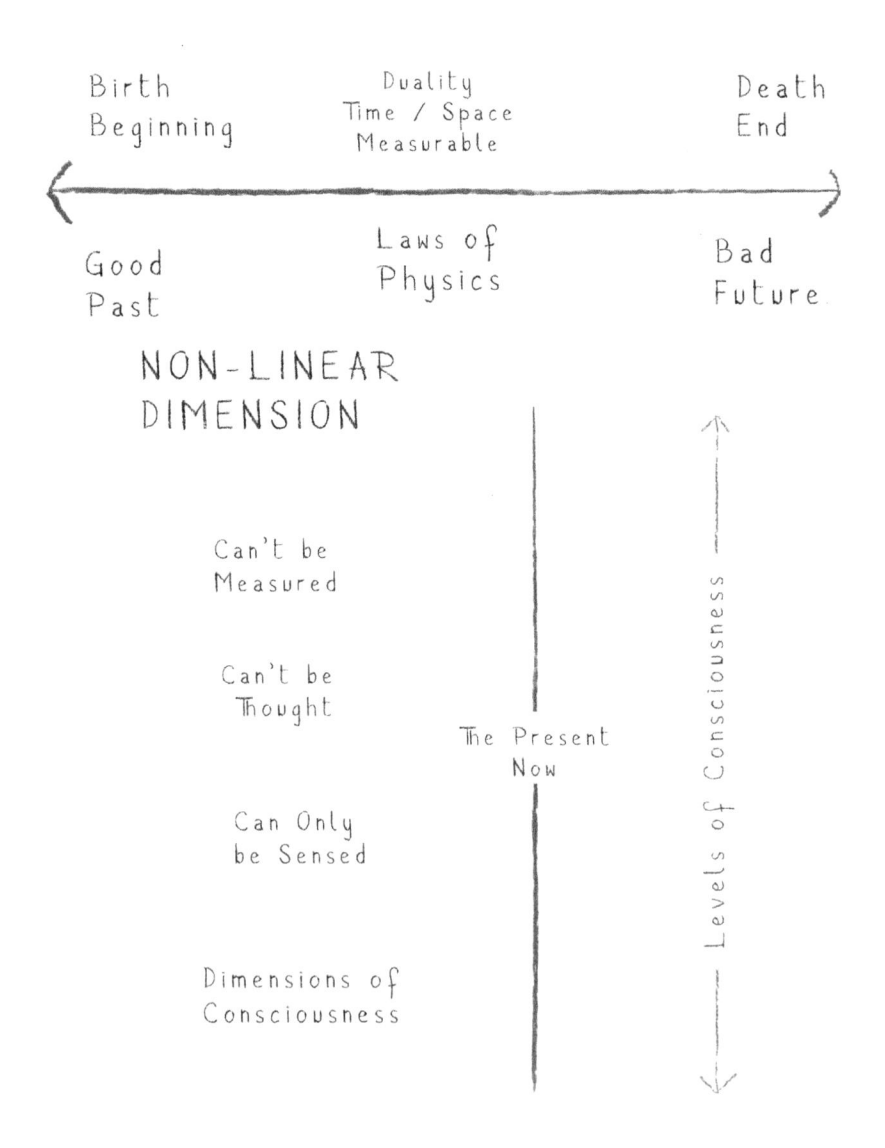

THE GIFT IN THE WOUND

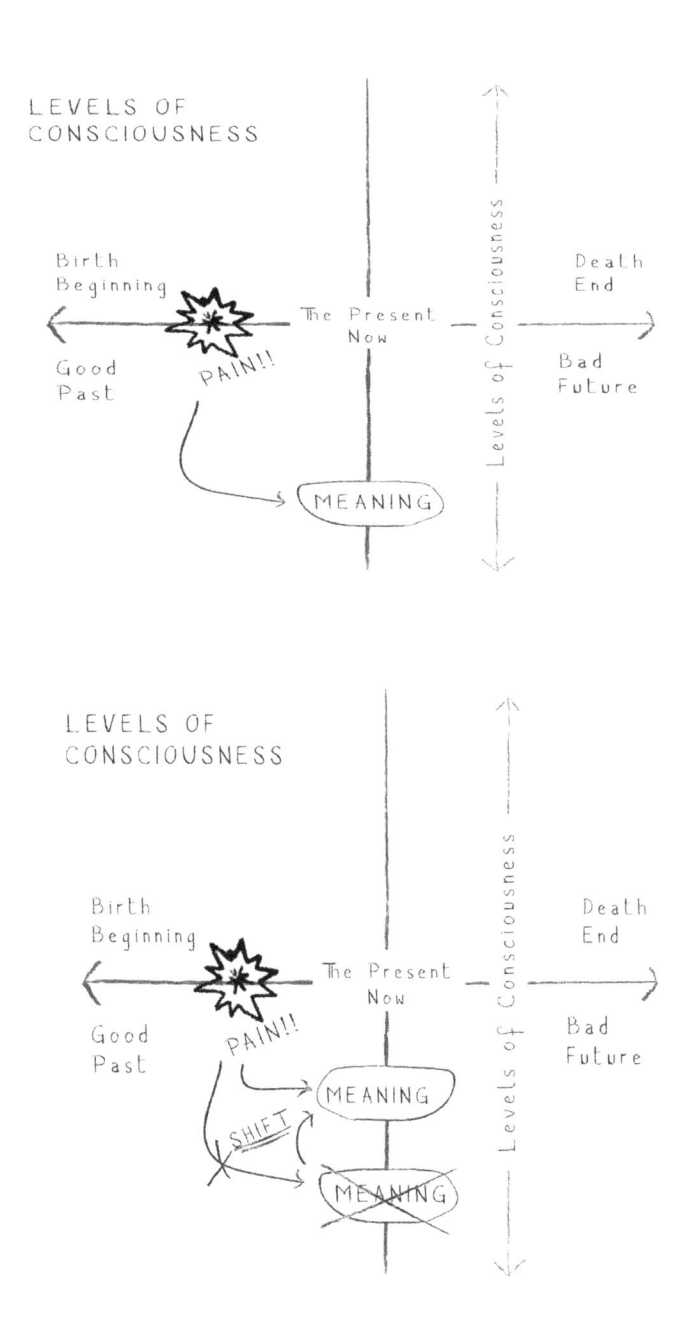

LEVELS OF CONSCIOUSNESS

Birth / Beginning
Good Past
PAIN!!
The Present Now
Death / End
Bad Future
Levels of Consciousness
MEANING

LEVELS OF CONSCIOUSNESS

Birth / Beginning
Good Past
PAIN!!
The Present Now
Death / End
Bad Future
Levels of Consciousness
MEANING
SHIFT
~~MEANING~~

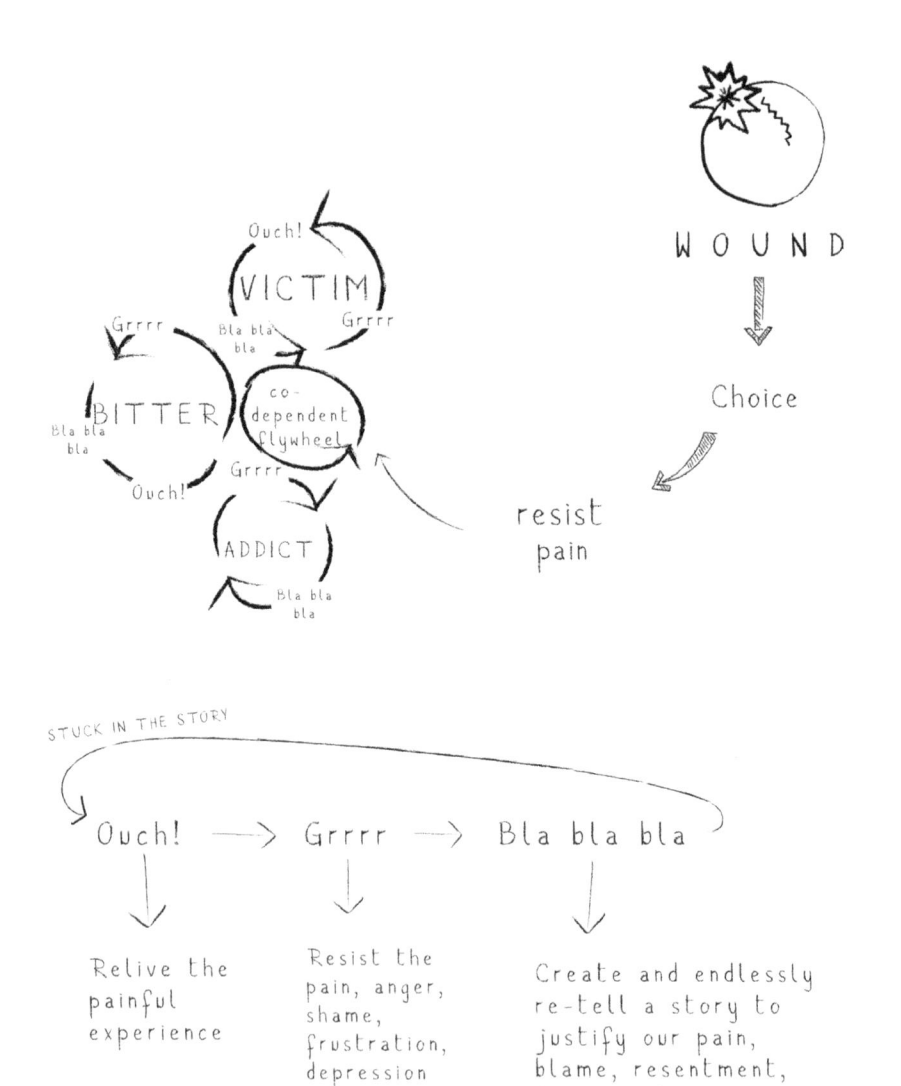

SECTION 2: TWO VIEWS OF REALITY: LINEAR AND NON-LINEAR

WOUND

Choice

resist pain

VICTIM
BITTER
ADDICT
co-dependent flywheel

Ouch! Grrrr Bla bla bla

STUCK IN THE STORY

Ouch! → Grrrr → Bla bla bla

- Relive the painful experience
- Resist the pain, anger, shame, frustration, depression
- Create and endlessly re-tell a story to justify our pain, blame, resentment, fault-finding, self-pity

THE GIFT IN THE WOUND

KEY 3
The Pain Portal

Understanding pain and its purpose requires moving into an uncomfortable, counter-intuitive space in our minds and considering ideas about ourselves, our purpose, and our life's experiences that we typically avoid altogether.

While the ultimate goal isn't necessarily to learn to love or seek out more pain, the concepts included in this key can help unlock the secret power of pain as the portal or gateway to healing and discovering the gifts in pain-ridden wounds.

The first concept related to Key 3 is understanding more precisely the different types of pain, their roots, and the role each plays in our approach to life experiences. Deeper understanding sharpens our ability to explore alternative approaches that can more effectively speed us along our journey.

In the next chapter, we'll apply our new understanding of paradox to the concept of pain. The pain paradox reveals a surprisingly simple, highly empowering "flip-side" insight that is often the turning point for many individuals in understanding their life's trials and the path forward.

The principles and progress described by Key 3 can be accelerated and enhanced by bringing what we call "militant healing" to the process. Mastering the paradox of pain requires great initial effort and will power – a type of militancy toward healing that this final chapter will illustrate.

THE GIFT IN THE WOUND

Pain And The Purpose of Pain

Though our natural instinct is to get rid of it, pain is the messenger for all emotional issues that we deal with and thus the portal to resolution of those issues.

Brad sat at his desk with his back to me as I entered the doorway. He was focused on the computer screen, intently reading. The room was warm and inviting. The walls and shelves were lined with poignant images, sculptures, quotes, and books that revealed deep thought and spiritual focus. I was amazed at the breadth of culture I had been exposed to in the short time I had known him. One day we'd be talking about wisdom literature from the Toltec mystics, the next day about some of the latest advances in psychological or neurological research, and then we'd be on to scripture and ancient Near-Eastern poets. Being in his office was to bathe in the best collection of knowledge from time immemorial to the present.

He turned around, stood, and greeted me pleasantly.

"So, what's on your mind today?" he asked as we sat down.

"From our last discussion, you said that everyone has a wound (or in my case, wounds). And every wound has a gift. But is seems to me that all this causes a whole lot of pain. And there seems to be a lot more pain than gifting going around. The gifts certainly haven't been obvious to me, but I'm drowning in pain. I'm not making the connection."

SECTION 2 : PAIN AND THE PURPOSE OF PAIN

> You would bring up that painful subject up right off the bat, he quipped with a twinkle in his eye. Pain is such an integral part of our existence, it has even been popularized to the phrase, 'life is pain.'

"That's clever and works in the movies, but begs the fundamental question," I returned. "Why pain?"

> I'm glad you asked, said Brad. It's true that every wound has a gift. But every gift is encased in a shell we've constructed that keeps it hidden from our consciousness. Ironically, you may soon discover that your pain is actually the key to uncovering that gift.

I looked at him quizzically, but he continued.

> The purpose of pain is to tell us that something is wrong, or out of harmony. At the biological and psychological level, our instinct is to move away from anything that is unpleasant. We don't have to consciously think, "I'm going to move away from pain." It's just a natural function to move away.

> The linear model of health, or curing, is to eliminate pain. The main reason people go to doctors is because of pain. We want to get rid of the pain because we're biologically wired to do that. But if we do that, we don't learn what the pain is telling us.

> To be able to know what pain is saying, it generally helps to talk about what types of pain we experience.

Types of Pain

Brad opened the white board behind the cabinet, and wrote,

"Types of Pain" with three bullets underneath.

Pain generally falls into one of three categories: physical pain, emotional or psychological pain, and spiritual pain.

Physical Pain. This type of pain is always held in the body. It is often associated with a malady or pathology the body is dealing with. But it can also be a manifestation of one of the other types of pain, and not linked to a specific pathology.

Emotional and Psychological Pain. Emotional pain comes from the meaning we put on any given condition or particular experience – our beliefs about that pain. For example, when a person's self-esteem is based on what other people think about them, the withdrawal of approval becomes devastating. We consciously apply meaning to many experiences, but more often we simply react with unconscious beliefs that we hold.

For example, you may have experienced a significant loss early in your life that has long been forgotten in the conscious memory. But when you have a similar experience later in life, those childhood beliefs influence how you react to the current loss.

People will often tell themselves that they shouldn't be feeling this sad or that they are silly for feeling so upset about something. We must realize that the brain keeps all data and interpretations of data until new meaning is put on the old traumas that are being triggered currently. If you are feeling something, there is a reason for it and it must be looked at. You must discern whether the pain is because of present circumstance or is something of the unresolved past.

SECTION 2 : PAIN AND THE PURPOSE OF PAIN

Probably the most problematic (and common) emotional or psychological pain comes to us when someone we care about stops loving us. Many of us believe we are less when we are unloved, and we need look no farther than pop music to see that. So much of our music and poetry centers on love lost and the pain associated with that experience. On a more dramatic scale, if someone believes that they are nothing without someone's love, being without romantic love has the potential of devastating them. This type of pain must be examined if we are to heal.

Spiritual Pain – The Worst, Brad wrote by the third bullet on the board. Spiritual pain is existential pain – the pain of our existence, our being, or our evaluation of ourselves. It is often fueled by serious fundamental doubts such as 'I don't know if there is a God,' 'I don't know what my purpose is,' or, 'I don't know why I am on the planet.'

Spiritual pain is the pain of loneliness, of purposelessness, of abandonment. It is the pain of feeling as if we don't have the skills, the tools, or the strategies to make our lives happy. It's the pain of life with no purpose – a type of nihilism for oneself. In some cases it leads to the ultimate rejection of the self, which is suicide. Spiritual pain is the pain of feeling disconnected from all valued relationships, including with oneself.

Of all the types of pain, spiritual pain is by far the most problematic because it comes down to the meaning and purpose of your existence. To address these issues requires a whole different set of tools and strategies.

I was writing as fast as I could to keep up with Brad's explanation.

Another deep spiritual pain, and often the most difficult to heal, is the pain that comes from neglect. Neglect says, 'Nothing happened, but it should have.' The brain and mind don't do well with 'nothing,' so they make it into 'something.' That something is often interpreted to mean something about the self: 'I'm not worthwhile or worthy or deserving of love'.

"Okay, three basic types of pain," I said, looking at the outline on the board. "But what about the scenario you referred to earlier where there are physical symptoms, but no pathology. There must be a fair amount of crossover," I suggested.

You're exactly right, Brad replied

All Pain is Connected

We separate types of pain in order to conceptually talk about them. But in reality, they can't be separated. They are all closely linked and interactive with one another. For example, spiritual pain will often manifest itself physiologically. Research studies have shown neglect to also have long-lasting biological significance on the heart and the brain.c

In fact, most physiological pain comes from one of the other areas. The problem is that in our linear thinking we've settled on the notion that we can treat all physical pain with things that rid us of symptoms: a pain killer, a surgical procedure, or a medical treatment.

With the linear medical model, if I go into a physician and say, "I'm depressed," there is no biological marker for depression, so he treats the depression with a physical modality – usually antidepressant or anti-anxiety medications. It's important to recognize that depression and anxiety are usually symptoms of something. They are messengers carrying an important message for the holder of the symptoms. To effectively address root causes, we shouldn't kill the messenger; we should try to understand the messages of the emotion.

In fact, there is a movement that says all physical pain is the result of an emotional upset. These symptoms are 'dis-ease' in the most literal sense of the word, meaning they are symptomatic of an underlying uneasiness with our emotions. And because the medical world generally does not view this understanding as scientific, we are often treating symptoms rather than getting to the root of the problem. When you deal with the emotional issues, the physical manifestation of pain goes away.

We see anecdotal evidence of this all the time. People 'heal' a relationship, and their physical symptoms disappear. People who have 'broken hearts' often deal with heart issues, as the heart is the center of all emotional relationships. They often feel unsafe and extremely vulnerable but have replaced those feelings with anger or some other kind of armor.

Rather than masking non-physiological symptoms with physiological treatments, the vast majority of these illnesses could be effectively treated by a lifestyle change or learning how to deal with the dark emotions, rather than merely turning our body over to the physician and saying, 'You cure me. You take away my pain.'

If we are experiencing physical pain, by all means a visit to the doctor is in order. But at the same time, we would be wise to look at emotional situations – conscious and unconscious

– that may be creating the pain and impacting physical health.

"Okay, so you're saying that traditional treatment might not always be the best option for much of the pain we experience in life. So how do we deal with it and get rid of it?" I probed.

Unfortunately, what you just said is a big part of the problem, Brad replied. If we are going to heal the pain, as counterintuitive as it may sound, the fundamental objective should never be to get rid of it.

"What do you mean, 'never to get rid of it?' Isn't that the objective of healing, to be freed from pain?" I asked.

Well, before we get to that - and we may not even be able to this session- we need to talk a little more about emotions and emotional pain.

"OK, I'm all ears," I said, turning another page on my pad.

Emotions

Everything in life is based on relationships – relationships to ourselves, to others, and to a higher power. Emotions are what define those relationships. They are simply messengers that give us information about what is going on in our environment, our relationship to that environment, and our relationship to our inner world.

Emotions are made up of complex hormones and chemicals created by the body for the purpose defining our relationships with our environment. They are not supposed to do anything of themselves, but are a result of the way we see the world.

For example, if we're anxious, its usually because there is an outcome we cannot control in our environment. If we're depressed, there is something in our environment that we have lost or that we are mourning. If we're afraid, there is something in our environment – either internal or external – that is threatening us. If we're angry, something in our environment has offended us deeply. If we are resentful, we are overestimating our own importance at the expense of another. If we are frustrated, a desire or want is not being met. These feelings don't have any inherent meaning; they simply give our mind crucial information on safety, security, and problem-solving.

Because they have no intrinsic meaning, emotions are neither good nor bad. They simply are. Good and bad are not feelings, they are judgements. There are pleasant emotions and unpleasant emotions, but just because they are unpleasant doesn't make them bad.

With the so-called dark emotions - depression, anxiety, anger, fear, jealousy and resentment – our natural behavioral and psychological instinct is to move away from them because they are painful and 'bad'. From this line of thought, it is easy to make the assumption that there are bad emotions and good emotions and thus try to eliminate them. But doing so defeats the purpose of those emotions, which is to tell us that we are experiencing some interaction with our environment.

Paradoxically, it's our resistance to the dark emotions that causes us so much psychic suffering.

A philosopher named Khalil Gibran summed up the purpose of emotions and pain in this insightful little couplet:

"Pain is the breaking of the shell that encloses our understanding."

So, to answer your original question, the purpose of pain, whether it is physical, emotional, psychological, or spiritual, is to open our understanding. That breaking open of the shell exposes an important choice we each must make, consciously or unconsciously, that determines the level of understanding we attain from dealing with the pain.

"So what's next?" I asked.

Keep peeling the onion. As you raise your level of consciousness in one area, it exposes the opportunity to heal other areas of pain in your life and relationships. Address the next most acute pain, and see if you can learn its message. Find the beauty in the painful healing process. And then we'll explore some ways to help you along the path of faith and healing.

There are a number of things you can do to help you in that process. The simplest is breathing as we've discussed a number of times already. Meditation is also a great option. There are a number of different types, but even basic mindfulness meditation can help put you in a mindframe that is conducive to aiding this journey.

I looked at my watch. Our time was gone, and we had barely started the discussion on how to heal all this pain. "Hmmm...we aren't going to get the healing discussion today, are we?" I suggested. "You know that will cause me a lot of emotional pain."

Well, that's neither good or bad, just something for you to sit with, he replied, closing the white board door. It may be a while before you are ready to understand how to heal from your pain. In the meantime, practice accepting it, rather than running away from it.

Notes From My Note Pad

The purpose of pain is to tell us something is wrong, out of harmony.

Biological and psychological instinct is to move away from pain.

Three types of pain:

Physical = pain held in the body

Emotional and Psychological = the meaning we put on any condition or experience = our perception or beliefs about that pain

Spiritual = the spiritual meaning of the purpose of our existence – who am I, why am I here, what is my reason for being on the planet

The pain of loneliness, not feeling purposeful or loved—the worst kind of pain

All three are closely linked and interactive

Most physiological pain comes from one of the others

Linear model of health or curing is to eliminate pain.

The problem: treat all pain with only a physical modality: drug, surgery, physical treatment

Pain is actually a symptom = a messenger with an important message: don't kill the messenger! Focus on healing, not getting rid of pain

Emotions: messengers that give us crucial information

Neither good nor bad. They simply are

Not problems: just because they are unpleasant doesn't make them bad

Dark emotions: painful; naturally want to move away/get rid of them

Pain is the breaking of the shell that encloses our understanding

Then we must choose to move into, embrace the pain and learn its message

Determines the level of understanding, depth of the gift we take from dealing with the pain

Bottom Line: the purpose of pain is to open our understanding to the gift that is in every wound.

SECTION 2 : PAIN AND THE PURPOSE OF PAIN

Quotes From My Quote Book

Everyone has a wound
Every wound has a gift
The deeper the wound, the greater the gift
Pain is the portal

"Pain is the breaking of the shell that encloses our understanding."

–Kahlil Gibran

The Pain Paradox

As we take a leap of faith and lean into our pain, we find that it has a personal message for us.

This time, when I came into the office there was little small talk. I could sense that Brad was very anxious to talk about whatever he had prepared.

> Today we talk about a choice that steers us away from dead ends and puts us on the path of healing and increasing consciousness. The path, coincidentally, is the mirror image of the path to the dead ends.
>
> The path to dead ends starts out easier, with choosing to avoid or ignore pain, but ends in the difficulties of victimization, bitter, and addiction. Because its beginning is naturally more comfortable, the vast majority of us initially steer that way and live in dead ends in various aspects of our lives.
>
> The path to healing is the more difficult initially because it begins with the counterintuitive notion of accepting or embracing our pain. But ironically, embraced pain carries the gift of virtually effortless healing that flows to us in the form of remembered wholeness, raised consciousness, and peace.

"Hmmm…," I mused. "If it's so difficult and counter to our natures, why would anyone want to face that suffering willingly?"

Initially, many are forced into it by the intensity of the pain or difficulty of circumstance. In those situations, we must face the pain and choose the meaning we will assign to it.

Recently a man came into the cancer group for the first time. Two months previously he had been diagnosed with a brain tumor. He had surgery and was undergoing radiation treatment. As a result, his cognitive function and speech had been severely affected. He said he was in constant anxiety even with medication. We talked about what having brain cancer meant to him, and he said he'd lost his life. In a sense, on that level, he absolutely had. On the linear, horizontal dimension, he had lost his life, or life as he had defined it. Through halting speech he told me, "I have no purpose in life now. I want to find purpose."

I suggested to him, 'Would you consider that your purpose is exactly what you are doing right now: Discovering meaning in your illness, in the losses of the physical and cognitive capacity of your body? Would you consider that that's your purpose?' In essence, I was inviting him to reconsider the meaning he was putting on an extremely painful experience on the linear dimension, to shift his awareness on the vertical dimension, and to choose a new, more enlightened meaning for experiences that were being measured, diagnosed, and treated on the horizontal dimension.

Something in him clicked. That realization not only raised his level of awareness, but it changed things on the horizontal/physical dimension as well. He looked better. His whole countenance changed.

We did a short group meditation. Afterward this man said, 'I've never felt this peaceful.' His whole physical countenance was changed. His ability to speak increased, and it wasn't because I had gotten used to how he spoke. His countenance, his whole affect, changed by shifting from what happened to him, being victimized by a disease, to sensing the possibilities on another dimension.

That transformation can happen instantaneously, or it can happen very slowly. But I believe it is always a possibility.

I was fascinated. How could anyone so incapacitated find peace in the middle of such a crisis? Was simply choosing to see it a different way really all it takes? I was thinking hard and writing furiously in my notebook. Seeing my engagement and willingness to understand, Brad continued.

The Paradox of Pain – Embrace Pain as the Messenger

In order to heal from pain, you must see the purpose of pain. If you see pain as something you just want to get rid of and has no purpose, it creates another set of problems. Pain without meaning is exquisite suffering. It causes us to ask the unanswerable and pain-inducing question, 'Why is this happening to me?' If you can't find meaning and purpose in pain, it's like not having any purpose in life. People who don't have purpose in life aren't on the planet very long. If they can't find some conscious reason to exist, they don't.

At a biological and egotistical level, pain – including the 'dark' emotions– is offensive, so we do everything we can to avoid it. We want to get rid of it, to eliminate it. When we are feeling misery, we just want it to end. So, we resist it. That's the natural psychological-biological inclination.

SECTION 2 : THE PAIN PARADOX

The key to healing is, ironically, a willingness to submit to the pain, to embrace it, to understand its message. Pain is the process that is telling us that there is something wrong. This kind of pain is absolutely necessary because it calls us back to start examining ourselves.

It's counter-intuitive – why would I do that? It doesn't make any sense. And the ethics of the medical model reinforce that thinking: get rid of it, medicate it, or fix it, but certainly don't embrace it. So we treat the symptom – the grief or the depression – but it is still there. It's just masked. It simply melts into the unconscious from which it came. It's never healed, because the emotion is only the messenger, pointing us to the root issue that needs to be healed.

If we merely rid ourselves of pain or dark emotions, we don't learn the message that each messenger is bringing. Our natural tendency is to kill the messenger before we hear the message.

Recently I was talking to a young woman who has been in the traditional medical psychotherapy model of healing for years.

'What's your diagnosis?' I asked.

'They've diagnosed me as bi-polar, borderline personality disorder, and a couple of other things,' she replied.

'How are they treating these "disorders"?

'With meds.'

'How many medications are you on?' I asked.

'Currently, about seven different meds,' she said.

I asked, 'Your doctors think that's the best plan?'

'Yes, they tell me I can't come off of them,' she replied

'And do you think that is the best plan for you?' I asked. 'Do they make the quality of your life better?'

'NO!' she answered emphatically.

I asked, 'You've been in this misery, this psychological suffering for how many years?'

'As long as I can remember,' she replied.

I gently probed further. 'Has anyone asked you the source of your pain? Was it an event? A process of invalidation? Was the pain physical, emotional, psychological or spiritual? Has anyone ever addressed the purpose of your pain?'

'I don't remember anyone ever asking me those questions,' she responded.

So I asked her, 'Has anyone ever asked you to see the purpose of your pain? Has anyone ever asked you to make friends with it, and to see what it is trying to tell you about your level of consciousness, about yourself, and the way you see the world?'

'That's stupid, why would I want this pain?'

'It's not that you want the pain, it's that your pain is there for a purpose, and you need to understand that purpose. It's telling you something about the nature of your life,' I suggested. 'It may be telling you that you really are worth something.'

'That's the stupidest thing I've ever heard,' she retorted.

Needless to say, we didn't make much headway in understanding and beginning to heal her pain.

This young lady had been holding a great deal of toxic shame from childhood experiences. She was living in a toxic marriage, had no self-esteem, and in fact held herself in contempt. In her mind she deserved no better. She was unwilling to see that these deep spiritual and emotional wounds were the source of her pain, and that medication was treating the symptoms, not the root of the problems.

I attempted to get her to see that the story she had adopted over the years might not have been entirely accurate and that choosing a new perception may serve her better. However, she was very reluctant to see pain as anything except pain, and the sole strategy in dealing with it was to make it 'go away' by medicating it.

Medication can be a great tool when it makes the quality of life better for the person taking it. But even when medication is working as a productive means, we tend to diminish its emotional and psychological benefits by ascribing the power of healing solely to the medications.

So often people give credit to the 'meds' for helping them, and feel ashamed because they must rely on them. There seems to be a real stigma for those who use medication to cope with depression or anxiety. The reality is, credit should be given to ourselves for having the wisdom to take the medications that aid our healing process. They are merely a tool to facilitate the process.

This is a perfect example of the way most of us have been programed to think. Creating distance from something unpleasant is our natural tendency. In fact, nature herself seems to have a resistance to change, even though nature is constantly in flux. It is our resistance to pain that creates the terrible psychic suffering that so many face. Learning to work with this resistance is most of the battle in dealing with something defined as unpleasant.

Unfortunately, much of our natural instinctual approach is reinforced through the linear scientific model, and more particularly, the linear medical model. If someone is told they need to take a nasty medicine or difficult treatment for a physical ailment, they say, OK, I'm willing to do that.

But if they are told they need to move into this difficult emotional situation and embrace their pain, it's so far out of their frame of reference that most people won't even consider it.

"So it's basically what people have been telling me for years: that after a mistake or painful experience, analyze it and try to find the life lesson in it," I suggested.

That's a good retrospective approach, and certainly can uncover a great deal of important insight. But a potentially greater opportunity for healing is to stay present, embrace pain in the moment, and discover its message.

"What do you mean, embrace the pain and discover its message?" I asked.

I mean that rather than reacting to the pain, stepping back and being the observer. I tell people it's like going on a safari or expedition, and coming upon this unusual, interesting, and highly emotional scene. Successful wildlife observers carefully track their game, and then with the greatest of patience, quietly wait and watch as the wonder of the scene unfolds before them.

In this case, instead of observing something or someone else, you are observing your own anger and your own emotional situation. In that moment you can say, 'That's really interesting that I'm so angry. I wonder what that's about. I think I'm going to sit and observe it and see what comes of it.'

As odd as it may sound, you can actually have a conversation with your pain, find out its purpose, and ask it to deliver its message.

"It almost sounds like you are having a conversation with a person," I suggested. "I don't mean to sound like your client on all the meds, but that sounds a little out there to me."

Well, deep pain not only has a message, but also usually has a name, stated as the erroneous belief or incongruity that the pain represents. Resistance to pain will always make it worse. And pain doesn't just go away. Remember, pain is a messenger, and it will keep trying to deliver its message until it has been heard, received, and acknowledged.

Another courageous client of mine had the same types of questions and doubts about healing pain you just expressed. Getting past the resistance to pain, and even being willing to accept and move into it is one thing. But to actually have a conversation with your pain? That seemed a little far-fetched to him.

As we spoke, I encouraged him to take the first step in the healing process, which begins with this simple, counter-intuitive thought: 'I am willing to deal with this pain. It has something to teach me.' That's the first big step – willingness.

Well, either because of his commitment to healing, or the overwhelming pain of his depression – or maybe a little of both – he decided to give it a try.

The next time we got together, I was anxious to hear his experience.

'Did you have a conversation with your pain?' I asked.

'I did,' he replied.

'And, what did you discover?' I queried.

'Actually, a number of things,' he said, with an excited look on his face.

'For some time I had been feeling depressed. Things weren't going well in my life, and I felt I was incapable of making good decisions and succeeding. My professional and financial worlds were taking a nose dive, and none of my efforts in that arena seemed to be going anywhere. I felt out of touch with my wife and my relationship with my children seemed distant and strained.

'One day my wife and I argued over my handling of counseling our son regarding some important school decisions. Our conversation got more and more tense, accusatory, and defensive. I got so angry I had to walk away. I steamed all day, boiling with anger and resentment. I already felt incapable as a breadwinner and husband. Now I felt my spouse was telling I was failing as a father as well. I felt stupid and worthless. And angry. Very angry.

But rather than act on that anger, this time I decided to take your advice, step back, observe, and see if I could actually talk to it and learn something from it, to sit with it, fully experience it and understand its message.

'So, I went to a quiet, dim room, sat comfortably, and initiated a short meditation. I started by breathing, clearing my mind, and focusing on the present, and especially on the pain and anger I was experiencing. For the first time I can remember, I actually was able to observe my pain in a different light – as something I am dealing with, rather than something that controls my life and emotions. It was like I was observing myself grappling with this pain.

'I discovered that, just like you said, it had a name. And I also discovered that the language of the conversation was pretty rough – probably because the pain was so deep and intense. My conversation with my pain went something like this:

Me: Okay, pain. Let's get on with this. I believe you have a message for me.

Pain: I do

Me: What's your name?

P: Damn Stupid

Me: What is your message for me?

P: To tell you that you are damn stupid

Me: For what purpose?

P: So you won't try things that will make you look stupid.

Me: What is the consequence of me looking stupid?

P: People will laugh at you, ridicule you, make fun of you, say you are stupid. I am to protect you from looking stupid.

Me: Yes, but I know I am brilliant and talented. Why would you want to tell me I'm stupid to protect me from looking stupid?

P: In order to not look stupid, you have to not try too hard, so you can prove you are incapable; otherwise, while you might succeed, you might also fail, and that would make you look really stupid – and you can't take that chance. So you have to try enough to not completely fail, and look stupid, but not try hard enough to run the risk of great success but even greater failure and greater stupidity.

Me: Thank you for saving that message for me all these years and delivering it to me today. Thank you for trying to protect me. But you see, I'm a grown man now, and I'm able to protect myself from people's opinions.

P: So, you don't need me anymore?

Me: No, I don't need you anymore. Is there a specific incident I should know about?

P: What happened doesn't matter. It's in the past. You don't need to know the specifics; you don't need to be protected anymore. I have to go now. You don't need me.

Me: Thank you. You may go. And you don't need to come back.

'Brad, it was almost surreal, but the change was evident and powerful. I felt the anger literally leave as I now saw myself through entirely new eyes. I recognized this deep-seated pain and anger for what it was: a defense mechanism from the past that was no longer a necessary part of my life. I felt liberated, free to stretch for my potential without fear of failure. It was the most incredible, joyful feeling. And I felt deep compassion for myself for all those years of suffering under this false notion of success.'

This man was able to heal his deep pain of many years by acknowledging it, allowing it to deliver its message, understanding its purpose, thanking it, and then dismissing it and asking it to not return again. Remember, once pain has fulfilled its purpose, it actually does heal and leave. Or more precisely, we have healed it because we now view it from a higher level of consciousness and greater understanding than the one that created it in the first place.

"So you don't just observe it. You actually have a conversation with it," I opined.

Often that's true, but it's not exactly the same for everyone. Not everyone will experience this vivid or personified interaction with their pain. For some, when they embrace and sit with the pain, when they invite and listen for understanding, the insights come as clear insights and meanings they had never considered before – totally new ways of understanding the meaning of their experiences. For others, it may come during periods of quiet reflection while driving or walking. Still others may have these realizations come to them as a result of contemplation following deep conversations or a particular interaction. But they all come because of willingness to acknowledge and accept the pain and its message. This is the higher level of consciousness we discussed earlier.

"So you're saying if I sit with my pain or anger, embrace it, fully accept it, and invite it to deliver its message, I'll be able to figure this out," I began.

No, that's not exactly what I'm saying, because you won't figure it out. This healing isn't something you figure out, think about, or fix. It's something that you sense and experience, in the moment, spontaneously. You don't sit down and plan it out and think about how to apply it. You invite the appropriate circumstances and it will come spontaneously, effortlessly.

But that's only after tremendous effort and courage to do what feels entirely counter-intuitive: to accept and embrace the pain and anger in the first place, and to be willing to believe that it has a purpose. You really must get militant about your healing.

That's why I call this the path of purpose. It is based on your willingness to believe that you are worthwhile. That you aren't broken. That you aren't a mistake. That maybe you're okay. That maybe you really are loveable.

And you have to believe that there really might be purpose in your pain. You have to be willing to make that choice.

Brad concluded, This sort of healing is called sensory healing. It's healing that effortlessly flows to you. You don't will it or force it. You create the proper environment and it comes to you.

I knew that was my cue. "So, my assignment for this week is to sit with my pain, discover its message, and sense its purpose and healing, right?"

Your willingness is admirable, Brad replied. But the process does require patience. Sometimes insights and healing happen quickly. Sometimes they come very slowly over weeks, months, and even years. The important thing is to be willing – militantly willing.

"You'll have to define what militant means in this context…" I began.

…Next time we meet, he finished without missing a beat.

"You are quick," I replied as we walked toward the door.

Notes From My Note Pad

This path is the paradoxical mirror image of the path to the dead ends.

Dead ends: starts out easier = avoid or ignore pain. Ends in harder victim, bitter and addiction.

The path of healing: much more difficult at first = starts with accepting/embracing our pain.

Paradoxically, embraced pain carries the gift of virtually effortless healing

Comes as remembered wholeness, raised consciousness and peace.

We're often forced to confront pain by difficult experiences

To heal from pain, must see the purpose of pain. If you just want to get rid of it, has no purpose, it creates another set of problems.

Pain without meaning is exquisite suffering.

The key to healing: willingness to submit to the pain

How: stay present, accept, move into, embrace pain in the moment, and discover its message.

Be the observer

Like a safari or expedition = observe your own anger or pain

"That's interesting – what's that about?"

Have a conversation with pain/anger = it has a message

If get rid of pain or dark emotions, don't learn the message that each brings

Natural reaction: kill the messenger before we hear the message!

SECTION 2 : THE PAIN PARADOX

It's counter-intuitive – why would I do that? It doesn't make any sense.

Healing: Sensory experience

You don't figure it out, fix it, think about it

You sense, experience it in the moment

Militant Healing = Strange choice of words to describe healing. Remind him to clarify.

Pictures From My Sketch Pad

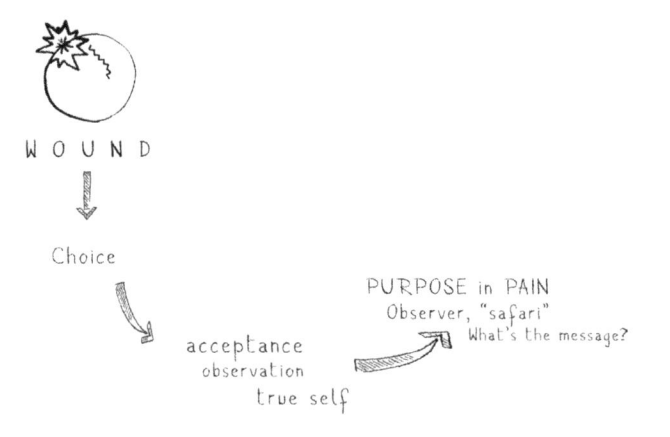

WOUND

Choice

acceptance
observation
true self

PURPOSE in PAIN
Observer, "safari"
What's the message?

Militant Healing

Diligently and consistently applying the principles of healing stops our cycle of victimization and changes our very nature.

I was tempted to dress in fatigues of some sort the next week to remind Brad of our topic of discussion, but I decided a more direct approach might get better results.

So, how was your week? Brad asked as we sat down.

"Well, for starters, I wasn't invited to participate in any militant healing demonstrations this week," I replied, sarcastically testing the waters a bit.

I can see you have a militant attitude about militant healing. You're not going to let me get sidetracked with other topics today, are you? he responded. That's good. You're displaying the type of tenacity that's the starting point for getting out of the story and on the path of effortless healing.

"Ok, shoot," I said, opening my note pad. "I mean, proceed. Go ahead. Enlighten me."

Brad smiled, leaned back, and began.

The word militant has developed a negative connotation because of what is happening in the world today. The news is full of examples of one group attempting to make its point with military violence against another. People are highly committed and passionate to the point that they are willing to die for a cause they believe is larger than themselves.

Militant healing means bringing the same kind of passion and commitment to the healing cause that others bring to a killing cause. Only a few things in life are worth dying for, yet people do it all the time to follow an ego-based, victimized view of the world.

While some things are worth dying for, healing is something worth living for. I encourage people to bring the same kind of passion and commitment to a healing cause as they bring to a dying cause. That cause is to heal their lives physically, emotionally and spiritually. It means being engaged with life at all levels.

Death comes to us all, but we have not failed because we die. Failure may be that while alive we really never lived.

"So you're talking about the really courageous part of beginning this journey, right?" I asked. "Like getting past the theory and ideas and actually facing your demons. I don't know about other people, but that's always been the hard part for me. I get the idea, and I'm willing to try. But I don't even know where or how to start."

Willingness & Militancy

You're not alone, Brad replied. A lot of people who start this journey say, 'I want to heal, but I don't know how to do this. I don't know how to start this journey.' While the task may seem daunting, at the biological level, saying this suggests to the brain that we don't know how to do something we actually intrinsically all know how to do.

It's like typing into a computer the search term, 'You can't find this information.' There's no possible way it will find it. The brain works the same way. The concept of willingness is absolutely the foundation of conscious change.

As we discussed earlier, the paradoxical nature of healing means dealing with discomfort, pain, and issues we are biologically and psychologically programmed to avoid and resist. It goes against our natural and domesticated instincts – which is why so many never undertake the healing journey in earnest.

The willingness to face and even embrace these issues is the starting point of being able to heal. If we are willing to begin, to entertain new, uncomfortable concepts, to embrace and submit, the 'how-to's' will come to us effortlessly and naturally from within. Without this willingness, the understanding of how to begin will never come.

Ironically, if we are given the 'how-to's' at the beginning of our journey, they are meaningless because of the absence of willingness that motivates us to consider their wisdom and worth. So what I'm saying is, you are already taking the first, biggest, and most important first step of willingness. You don't need to worry about a lot of the 'How do I do this?' and 'What's next?' It will come to you instinctually.

"Here's perhaps an extreme example of how healing can be intuitive," Brad offered, "from the life of a client of mine named Chris."

SECTION 2 : MILITANT HEALING

Unstoppable Chris

When I first met Chris, he was the epitome of a hard-driving, highly successfully man's-man who went after, and usually got, everything he wanted. He went to the gym at 4:30 every morning to build his body to perfection. He took body-building supplements, including testosterone, which not only built his physique, but made him hyper-sexual. While married and raising several children, he engaged in a number of extra-marital affairs.

He was a highly successful businessman who knew how to build a company and make a profit. Most people described him as just plain abrasive, and while they respected his business ability, no one really wanted to work with him or for him.

Over the years of hard-charging lifestyle, his relationship with his wife and family suffered significant neglect as he focused on other priorities in life.

Then, in an instant, his world changed. Driving home from work one night, Chris was struck at high speed on his motorcycle. He survived the crash, but not by much. He was stabilized at the scene, rushed to the hospital and given every lifesaving measure available. Despite the best medical efforts, he was left paralyzed from the neck down.

Lying in halo traction, unable to move, Chris was essentially forced into a nine-month meditation. Over those painful days and months, he was faced with the realization that he had lost everything, including the use of his body. He watched his beautiful physique melt away, and his 'perfect' world crumble. The final blow came when his wife informed him she was unable to continue to bear up under the strain of his tragic life, and she was taking the kids and leaving him.

Everything he had valued and worked so hard for had vanished, and he was totally helpless to change any of it.

Brad briefly paused before continuing:

Wading through the depths of despair day after day, often wishing there were a way he could end his misery, he slowly realized there was one thing he still had, that couldn't be taken away from him: his indomitable drive. It occurred to him that maybe the drive that had taken him down so many destructive paths could be the force to overcome his daunting challenges and take him on a healing path. He decided to give it a shot. What else did he have?

He had discovered the militancy for his own healing journey. Applied patiently one step at a time, his passionate drive opened to him a whole new world of sensory understanding, deep relationships, and love. It became the steady, energizing force that allowed him to heal and succeed at what had always been most important in his life, but had been brushed aside as weak and effeminate.

When I saw Chris a number of months later, he had recovered some use of his body and was learning to walk again. He had started a new business. But more than that, he was a very different man than the Chris I knew prior to the accident. If I had told you he was one of the most abrasive, abusive people I have known, you would have had a hard time believing me. Yes, there was a certain austerity about him, but abrasiveness had been replaced with militancy and channeled his energy toward healing, inner harmony, and love rather than feeding a nearly boundless ego intent on crushing anything in its way. An inner peace, quiet confidence, and sincerity of spirit were evident in his countenance and manner. Chris had discovered the power of militancy and healing.

There was silence as I sat deep in thought, processing what Brad had just laid out for me. This was a very different sort of militancy than what I had initially envisioned.

What's Your Spark? – Getting Un-Stuck From the Story

You were asking a while back about being stuck in the story, and how to break out of the cycle, Brad's strong voice broke the silence of my thoughts. It all begins with a spark of militancy.

For most militant causes, there is one small, determined action that sets things in motion. It's the event that everyone points to and says, 'That was the ignition point that started it all.' For example, the 'shot heard 'round the world,' or the bridge to Selma, or the Dandi Salt March.

They are relatively small incidents in comparison to what they eventually spawn. But they are the crucial, decisive ignition points that turn things upside down and set things in motion for massive, lasting change.

It's like one tiny spark that briefly flares into existence in a brilliant flash of light. An exertion of energy is required to produce it, yet it lasts only momentarily. But that spark has the power to ignite the flames of lasting impact that change lives and literally shape history.

So you must ask, 'What is my spark? What is that one small thing I can look to, that I can believe in, that I can hope for that will ignite the flames of militancy toward my own healing?'

Producing that spark requires effort. It requires choice. It requires that you get really disciplined about believing that it's worth it, that you're worth it. That maybe you're actually loveable. That maybe it's not totally crazy to believe that the pain has a message for you, something to teach you. And that as counterintuitive as is sounds, maybe there is something to be gained from embracing and accepting pain rather than resisting and masking it.

It's the militancy to take the first steps onto the path of purpose rather than the path of fear.

That spark of belief can interrupt the victim cycle when the painful memories of betrayal, disappointment, failure, and regret begin to melt yet again into anger, depression and blameful storytelling. It's the militancy to say, 'I will no longer choose to be the victim, to repeat the same stories of blame and shame about the same people who are no longer a part of my life. I choose to believe that there is purpose in my pain, and that I can discover and heal it.'

Sometimes sparks sputter. Sometimes they get rained on or blown out by wind. They may have to be re-ignited multiple times. Sometimes we must shelter them and gently blow on them to get them to ignite.

Militancy is required to recognize that breaking this cycle may not happen on the first attempt. Or the second, or the twenty-second. But persistence in pursuing belief in the intuitive

SECTION 2 : MILITANT HEALING

nature of healing will at one point give way to effortless healing and joy.

I jumped up, opened the white board, and quickly sketched the victim cycle we had discussed earlier. "So, you're still going to feel the pain, the Ouch! that's the first step in the victim cycle. It's re-living the pain of the experience that put us into feeling like a victim in the first place."

That's right, Brad replied.

"But before moving into Grrrr, into resisting the pain, you're saying light a spark right here," I said, drawing a spark-like figure between Ouch! and Grrrr. "It's a spark of hope. A spark of determination. A spark of belief that maybe there is purpose in my pain. Or maybe even purpose in my life. That maybe I'm worth it.".

Exactly, Brad interjected. It's that 'aha!' moment of belief, of faith, of hope.

I wrote "Militant Healing" by the spark and drew an arrow to the next step of a new cycle. "So rather than resist the pain, we're going to embrace the pain," I continued, "which is going to hurt like crazy." I labeled the next step OOOuuuch!

Brad chuckled. That's because initially it's so counter to our natures. It's like being told to run into the fire. I wrote "Run into the fire" below OOOuuuch!

The amazing thing is, that by embracing the pain, by running into the fire, we experience the next step, which is effortless healing, peace, and joy, Brad continued. I drew an arrow and labeled the next step "Ah" and wrote "effortless healing, joy" below it. It's very real, but a topic we will discuss and discover more as you continue your healing journey, Brad concluded.

Remember, this is not a spark to figure it out or fix it. It's not a spark to fight it, beat it, or get through it. Unlike the physical model of receiving and filling prescriptions, healing ideas goes beyond what you can think. Militant self-value helps you create a situation where you can sense it. Perhaps you use a thought process to get there, but when you sense it, a completely different experience emerges. You will sense wholeness and wellness. Answers and insights flow instinctively, effortlessly.

I closed my notebook, stood and saluted. "Yes sir! I'll do my best, sir."

Brad gently laughed, shook my hand and guided me toward the door. Your demons don't stand a chance with that kind of willingness.

Notes From My Note Pad

The word militant: negative connotation

People who are committed and passionate = willing to die for a cause bigger than themselves.

Militant healing: bringing the same passion and commitment to the healing cause that others bring to a killing cause.

SECTION 2 : MILITANT HEALING

Healing is something worth living for.

Life is sacred; most people don't want to die. But most people don't want to live with the level of militancy required to heal!

Willingness to face/embrace hard issues = starting point to heal.

Getting unstuck

Breaking into the cycle with the idea/spark:

Maybe there is purpose in pain, it has a message for me

Maybe I'm loveable; I'm worth it

Break in between "Ouch" and "Grrrr"

Unlike physical model of curing, healing ideas are beyond what you can think.

Create a situation where you can sense it.

Answers and insights flow instinctively, effortlessly; Will sense wholeness and wellness

GET REALLY MILITANT ABOUT YOUR HEALING!

Quotes From My Quote Book

"Militant healing means bringing the same kind of passion and commitment to the healing cause that others bring to a killing cause. Only a few things in life are worth dying for. Healing is something worth living for. Yet most people won't live with the level of militancy required to truly heal."

– C. Bradford Chappell

Pictures From My Sketch Pad

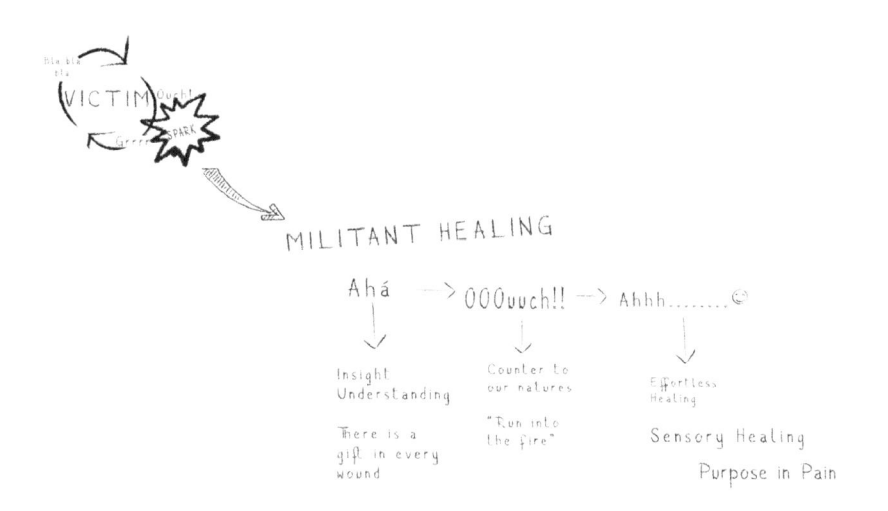

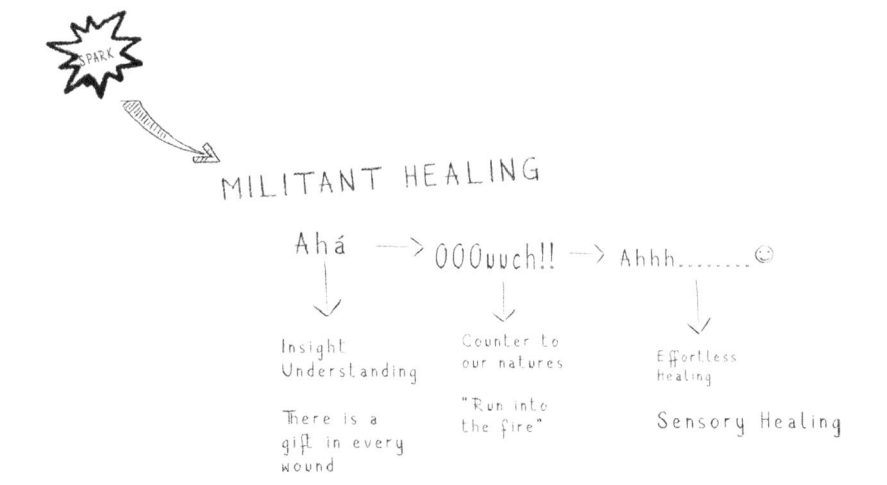

KEY 4
I Love Me

This key focuses on two powerful concepts that help us complete the healing journey of gift discovery. While certainly not new, in this context we explore them from the perspective of building on the previous keys and combining the resulting collective insights to move to the next level of understanding and empowerment.

With both concepts, the focus is on what may again be a counter-intuitive approach for many: to first love, accept, forgive and be grateful for self, and for your own unique journey and experiences in life. This is to not ignore the importance of including others in the mix, but the initial focus is "I love me."

The first concept included in Key 4 is gratitude. As applied to the framework, it represents a form of embracing or accepting our pain and the outcomes of our choices in life. Both of seeing the purpose in it all and sensing gratitude for the wisdom and insight.

The second concept centers on forgiveness. This chapter again focuses on forgiving self as a form of self love, and then forgiving others so that we can move on in our personal journey.

Gratitude

As we give thanks for every experience, we find natural joy and peace.

For the next couple of weeks I really focused on recognizing my victim stories and observing the pain point that initiated the stuck-in-the-story cycle. As I observed – sometimes with the help of my wife pointing out my bla-bla-bla phase – I was able to identify that spark point of militant faith or hope of a different outcome by moving into my pain and learning its message. I worked at it, but progress was slow and sometimes confusing.

I was anxious to meet with Brad again for some fresh perspectives on how to move forward.

So, how did your militant attitude toward healing serve you? he asked as I sat down across form him.

"Interestingly difficult," I replied. "I discovered a spark, but now it seems like there is even more pain to deal with. I moved past Oooouuuch to Ooooouuuuuuuuuch!"

I hear you. Breaking out of our victim story doesn't eliminate the pain. As we spoke about last time, it's like the spark that stokes the fires of commitment, but can seem to also stoke the fires of pain that you then are supposed to run into. Moving into or embracing our pain can be excruciating.

SECTION 2 : GRATITUDE

Here's a thought: Think about the wound, the painful experience, and tell me something you can be grateful for in it.

I stared at Brad like he was from another planet. Was he kidding?

"Grateful for?" I asked, half-calling his bluff. But I could see by the look in his eyes he was dead serious.

"What do you mean, grateful for? I thought I was trying to move into this pain, embrace it and understand it, but not be *grateful* for it. Besides, what in the world would I find to be grateful for in this unfair experience that totally messed up my life?"

Many people discover that militancy begins to break us out of being stuck in the story. But the next question is, what do we break into? What is the first step onto the healing path once we recognize the need to break out of the story?

Gratitude can be a step that helps accelerate moving onto the healing path by moving into your pain in another way. It's like having a target to aim for in landing on the path of faith.

You see, gratitude is actually a way of embracing the pain, of being open to discovering its story. What could be more painful than finding gratitude for your most trying, frustrating experiences? What could be more challenging than finding gratitude for those who have harmed you, abused you, or used you for their own selfish purposes?

Finding gratitude in a painful experience can give you something clear to focus on when igniting the spark of militant faith. This is a way of taking that momentum and breaking into the healing path.

THE GIFT IN THE WOUND

I was trying very hard to grasp what Brad was proposing here, but this was a big step for me. Finding something to be grateful for in these painful wounds seemed more like a forced exercise in futility than a healing step.

Brad let me sit with it for a few minutes. Finally I said, "Okay, let me share a story with you. One I read a number of years ago that has both inspired and puzzled me. It's about two women and their experiences in Nazi concentration camps.

"Corrie Ten Boom and her sister Betsie were Christians living in Holland at the time of the Nazi invasion. They took compassion on some of their Jewish neighbors and hid them in their house for a number of months. When they were ultimately discovered, the Ten Boom sisters were shipped off to the camps along with their Jewish friends.

"After spending time in two different camps, they were transferred to the most gruesome, disgusting camp yet. Wondering how they would survive, Betsie had an idea.

"From a verse in the Bible, she became convinced that the key was to give thanks in all circumstances. As they stood in the foul-smelling half light of this new filthy barracks, Betsie suggested they start the exercise immediately, by giving thanks for every single thing about the new dormitory.

"Corrie was incredulous. 'Such as?'

"'Such as being assigned here together. Such as the Bible you are holding in your hands.'"

"'Yes, thank you dear Lord that there was no inspection when we entered here. Thank you for all the women, here in this room, who will meet You in these pages.'"

"'Yes,' said Betsie. 'Thank you for the very crowding here. Since we're packed so close, that many more will hear.' She looked at Corrie."

"'Oh, all right. Thank you for the jammed, crammed, packed, suffocating crowds.'"

"'Thank you,' Betsie went on sincerely, 'for the fleas and for – '"

"The fleas! This was too much. 'Betsie, there's no way even God can make me grateful for a flea.'"

"'Give thanks in all circumstances,' Betsie quoted. 'It doesn't say "in pleasant circumstances." Fleas are part of this place where God has put us.'"

"And so they stood between piers of bunks and gave thanks for fleas. But this time Corrie was sure Betsie was wrong."

"In these incredibly trying circumstances, one of the few bright spots that kept them going were informal 'services' Betsie and Corrie held each night. Any kind of gathering, and particularly any religious 'service' was expressly forbidden and severely punished by the guards.

"At first, Betsie and Corrie called these meetings with great timidity. But as night after night went by and no guard ever came near them, they grew bolder. In the main assembly area they were under constant surveillance. It was the same in the main barracks: half a dozen guards or camp police always present. Yet, in the large dormitory room there was almost no supervision at all. They did not understand it. Soon, so many women wanted to join that they held a second service. These were services like no others. A single meeting night might include a recital of the Magnificent in Latin by a group of Roman Catholics, a whispered hymn by some Lutherans, and a sotto-voice chant by Eastern Orthodox women. With each moment the crowd would swell, packing the nearby platforms, hanging over the edges, until the high structures groaned and swayed.

"At last either Betsie or Corrie would open the Bible. Because only Hollanders could understand the Dutch text, they would translate aloud in German. And then they would hear the life-giving words passed back along the aisles in French, Polish, Russian, Czech, back into Dutch. They were little previews of heaven, these evenings beneath the light bulb.

"A number of days later, because of illness Betsie was assigned to the 'knitting brigade,' sitting in the sleeping rooms and knitting socks. Betsie was a lightning-fast knitter and completed her quota of socks before noon each day. She kept the contraband Bible with her, and spent hours a day reading from it to the other prisoners, moving from platform to platform.

"Then one evening Corrie returned to the dormitory to find Betsie excited, her eyes twinkling. 'You know we've never understood why we had so much freedom in the big room? Well, I found out.'

"'This afternoon,' she said, 'there was a confusion in her knitting group about sock sizes, and we asked the supervisor to come in and settle it. But she wouldn't. She wouldn't step through the door, and neither would the guards. And you know why? Because of the fleas! That's what she said, "That place is crawling with fleas!"'"

"Corrie's mind rushed back to their first hour in that dormitory. She remembered Betsie's bowed head, remembered her gratitude for creatures Corrie could see no use for."

I stopped and Brad stared at me intently.

"I've always thought that was an amazing experience," I said. "I sincerely appreciate and totally respect Betsie's story. But it's so extreme, it's always been a little hard for me to make the connection to my own situation."

Brad thought for a moment, swiveled around in his chair and pulled a well-worn book from the packed bookcase behind him. He flipped to a page and gazed at it thoughtfully before continuing. His eyes sparkled as he spoke. Many years ago, a poet by the name of Kabir wrote a wonderful poem entitled, "I Had to Seek the Physician":

*I had to seek the Physician
because of all the pain this world
caused
me.*

*I could not believe what happened when I got there –
I found my
Teacher.*

*Before I left, he said,
"Up for a little homework, yet?"
"Okay," I replied.*

*"Well then, try thanking all the people
who have caused
you pain.*

*"They helped you
come to
me."*

Brad closed the book and sat in silence as the words sunk in.

Suddenly, it all came clear. I was sitting here, walking this transformative healing path that was bringing such illumination and direction to my life because of the deep wounds and pain I had suffered. Without them, I would still have been spinning around in my own dead ends, oblivious to the opportunities for healing all around me. It was my need to seek the physician that was handing me and opportunity to heal a life of depression, blame and guilt; to find hope and meaning in life again; to discover and honor my genuine, authentic self.

I looked at Brad, and gratitude spontaneously swelled up in my heart. An overflowing warmth and joy swept over me, washing away the resistance, anger and confusion that had recently clouded my path. For a moment, time was suspended and it was as if I simultaneously sensed the accumulation of the collective wisdom Brad shared with me that had provided such poignant insights – wisdom of the sages, both past and present, classical training, powerful experiences of clients, and most importantly, wisdom from his own personal healing journey – all funneled to me and shared at the appropriate cross roads of my journey.

I couldn't believe I was actually sensing gratitude for being hurt, and for going through so much pain.

Brad sensed my awakening and deep gratitude. Before I could say anything, he stood and walked me to the hallway. Try finding gratitude for a few more wounds in your life, he suggested. You may discover that in reality, each does carry a healing gift. You may even discover gratitude for a few 'fleas' you thought served no purpose. He smiled as he shook my hand warmly.

I stood there speechless. But nothing needed to be said. As we parted, we both sensed the profound gift the physician had imparted that day.

Notes From My Note Pad

Gratitude can be a first step or "target" on the healing path as we break out of the dead end

Finding gratitude = a form of moving into the pain: "I'm grateful for all these people who hurt me!" (sounds super painful)

Betsie Ten Boom and the fleas – kept the guards away

The Physician = all this pain brought me here

I'm so grateful!

THE GIFT IN THE WOUND

Pictures From My Sketch Pad

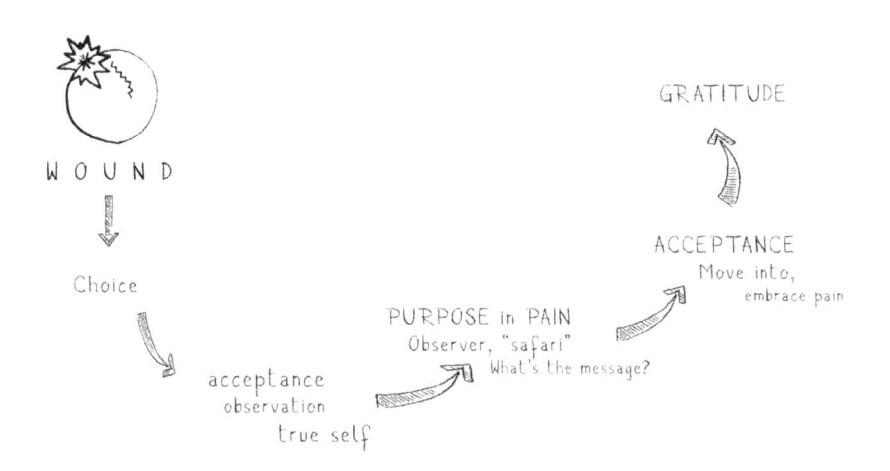

WOUND

Choice

acceptance
observation
true self

PURPOSE in PAIN
Observer, "safari"
What's the message?

ACCEPTANCE
Move into,
embrace pain

GRATITUDE

SECTION 2 : FORGIVENESS

Forgiveness

Forgiving those who least deserve it frees us from crippling anger and pride.

"Our discussion about gratitude last time has really changed my perspective and approach to the healing journey," I began as we sat down at the next meeting. "It's like a whole new layer of depth and meaning to a concept that I had just been walking right past for much of my life. I'm wondering what else I may have been missing that is a pivotal part of the process."

Well, here's one to try on, Brad replied.

Another way of focusing our militant healing toward the healing path is through forgiveness. Like gratitude, forgiveness is a form of embracing or accepting our pain. What can be more painful than forgiving the perpetrators of our deepest wounds? Worse yet, what can be more painful than forgiving ourselves for mistakes that we have made, knowingly or unknowingly? It requires us to take the counter-intuitive step of embracing this pain.

"I totally get the hard part of forgiveness," I ventured. "It always seemed like I was *supposed* to forgive, something expected of me, but I could never understand exactly *why*. As you describe it now, I can see that it's a way of moving into our pain."

Very true, but there are actually two facets to forgiveness. The obvious is to forgive others. Less intuitive, but probably more important, is the need to forgive ourselves.

"Yeah, I hear people mention that a lot: 'Now you need to forgive yourself.' It sounds like the harder of the easy-to-say/hard-to-dos."

In that case, let's start with the easier of the harders, Brad quipped.

Forgiveness of Others

Numerous authors, backed by extensive research, have established the many benefits of forgiving others. The powerful healing effects of forgiveness are well documented. The more difficult question is, 'How do I forgive? It's so difficult and painful, and seems so unfair.'

The starting point, and most important factor, is willingness! Willingness is the key that unlocks the door of our resistance to letting go of a hurt. It's the courage to embrace the pain of an experience and believe that there can be forgiveness.

A while back you described your discovery of the power of forgiveness in resolving the paradox of your rogue partner," Brad said.

"Absolutely! Once I got out of the 'should,' or expectation that I must forgive, I was able to understand that we forgive out of the desire to stop re-living the injustice done to us, not because the other person deserves or 'needs' to be forgiven," I replied.

That's a great insight in discovering the power of forgiving others, Brad said. Forgiveness is not something we do, it's the result of something, and it brings compassion, understanding, empathy to any given situation. Because of that, when you focus on forgiveness, you can't forgive.

And speaking of loving ourselves, it turns out that self-forgiveness requires a different approach.

"How is that?" I inquired.

Forgiveness of Self

Forgiveness of self is another matter. It requires honest acknowledgement of limitations and accountability. When you injure yourself you are both victim and victimizer. When you injure others you also injure yourself.

No one I have worked with over the years has every started out with the conscious intent to harm themselves or others. And yet everyone I have worked with has at some time harmed themselves or harmed others. Harm to ourselves usually comes in the form of self-deception, meaning that we unconsciously punish ourselves for perceived wrongs. When realized, it often creates a pain that permeates the soul. Often, this psychological violence we do to ourselves is seen as justification for sins and wrongs committed. Such was the case of an incredibly courageous woman I worked with named Susan.

When Susan was 19 she was abused by a trusted relationship, leaving her feeling ruined and worthless. She went on to marry a man who abused her physically, emotionally, and spiritually. She stayed because that was her 'just reward for being naive and stupid.' She was neither, but in her mind that was the truth.

She had four children with this man and often stood between him and his children to protect them from his insanity. She took beatings for the children or because of them. It was never exactly clear why. She prayed every day that he would disappear. Then one day, the man suddenly fell dead from a heart attack.

Six months after he passed away, Susan's daughter was cutting a horse out of a wire fence from which it had become entangled, was kicked in the head by the frightened animal, and died. This event Susan interpreted as just punishment for her unworthiness and that she should never be happy or find any peace from her existence.

"Wow, that's pretty harsh self-judgment," I observed. "And not based at all on truth."

People with consciences seem to take the task of self-punishment very seriously. They often use the tools of rationalization and justification for their self-punishment. The irony is that these are the same tools used by people who are unwilling to take any accountability for their attitudes and behaviors.

In the Judeo-Christian philosophy, sin is a big part of the dogma. Sin in the western culture has come to mean that one is not in good standing with God, and that God has somehow withdrawn His approval of the sinner. Paul put us all in the category of sinners when he said "that all have sinned and come short of the glory of God." (Romans 3:23, King James Translation)

In the original Greek, the word for sin was "hamartia." Although it refers to catastrophic failure, literally translated it means, "to just barely miss the mark," as in archery. From this definition we can see the truth in Paul's statement, because all of us have "missed the mark" in some way, no matter how small. However, it does not mean that we judge and condemn ourselves unmercifully or ever withdraw approval from ourselves.

Tragically, that is how many of us learned to motivate ourselves. We learned disapproval because we were disapproved of, and we came to identify with the disapproval, to believe that we *were* the mistake, rather than understanding that our failure meant, 'It just didn't work for me.'

Forgiving self requires us to admit that we have limitations. It requires us to admit that we don't know everything, we don't understand everything even though we are 'supposed' to know and understand. It requires true vulnerability.

Susan was one who displayed this vulnerability. Her healing was a slow and gradual process. The strengths that helped her survive some extremely difficult life trials also helped in her healing journey. For example, her anger that was turned inward, and her defiance toward her husband's abuse served her well in her militant commitment to caring for herself.

She joined a gym and was extremely diligent in disciplining herself to lose the weight that she had used for armor and protection. She was willing to embrace her vulnerability to do body work, releasing the toxins that had been stored there, creating health challenges.

Over time, Susan began to accept and honor who she genuinely was: an incredibly strong, talented and intelligent woman, not the mistake she had come to believe she was. She focused on an amazing, latent creative artistic talent, particularly in sculpture inspired by her deep affinity for animals. She naturally related more with the four-legged animal kingdom than she did with the two-legged kind, and often said in session that humans are not to be trusted because they wear masks and are so often dishonest in their relationships. With an animal, what you see is what you get.

Now there are many times in her life that she finds joy and happiness – sometimes in the achievements of her children, sometimes as she works with her animals, and at other times, in her work as an artist. She is reaping the sweet fruits of self-forgiveness.

"Powerful stuff," I replied. "It's a little counter-intuitive that forgiveness, like gratitude, is more than just a desirable virtue. They are actually important steps along the healing path."

Very true, Brad replied. But it's important to remember that we are dealing in the sensory realm here, not the linear world. So one doesn't necessarily come before the other. You don't have to have gratitude before you experience forgiveness, and vice-versa.

Nor are they mutually exclusive, or exclusive of other healing modalities. But they do provide important opportunities to focus and accelerate our healing journey.

"Thanks for today's insights, Brad," I replied as I closed the notebook. I stood and gazed out the window for a moment. "It all seems so clear when we are talking here. But it seems to fade when I leave. It's such hard work, and can be so confusing."

That's the hard inner work that makes all the difference, Brad replied. The vast majority of people on the planet shy away from the pain and commitment required for the healing journey. As a result, they also miss out on the peace and transcendent joy available in any life circumstance to those willing to pay the price.

"I'm willing. I'll keep working at it," I replied resolutely.

That's the choice that is so important in the journey, Brad returned. If you stick with it, your level of consciousness and understanding will increase, and you will discover that you've actually made more progress than you may have thought.

I walked to the car with that hope brimming in my heart.

Notes From My Note Pad

Forgiveness is a way of moving into our pain

It's one of the most powerful ways to discover the gift in the wound

Two types of forgiveness: others; self

First requires willingness

Forgiveness is not something we do, it's the result of something.

If focus on forgiveness, can't forgive

Forgive not because they deserve it. But because you love yourself so much

THE GIFT IN THE WOUND

We take self-punishment seriously - use rationalization and justification (same tools used by people unwilling to be accountable).

Sin has come to mean "catastrophic failure"

How we motivate ourselves: we were disapproved of, therefore we are the mistake vs. it didn't work for me

Requires true vulnerability – e.g. admit you don't know even though you are supposed to know.

Requires brutal honesty with self – requires us to be authentic.

Forgiveness is symbolic letting go

Allows us to let go of what we are holding onto in the linear world

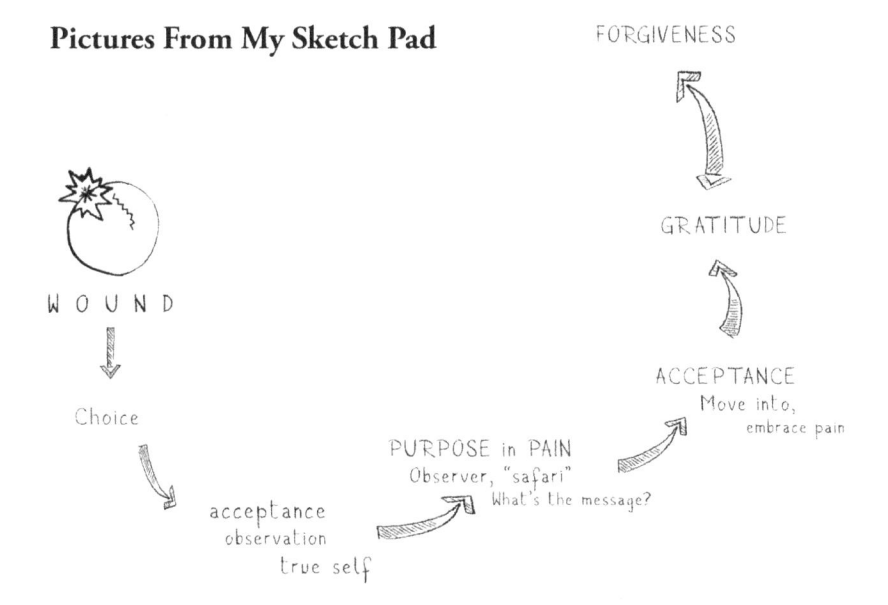

Pictures From My Sketch Pad

FORGIVENESS

GRATITUDE

W O U N D

ACCEPTANCE
Move into,
embrace pain

Choice

PURPOSE in PAIN
Observer, "safari"
What's the message?

acceptance
observation
true self

KEY 5
Effortless Acceptance

The fifth key continues the vein of often counter-intuitive insights. Since this is symbolically the latter stage of the discovery journey, we might be inclined to push hard, make that final effort, and sprint for the finish.

This key uncovers the often-misunderstood concept of effortless acceptance. While earlier keys – particularly Key 4 – required significant effort, courage, energy and commitment, this key outlines the beautiful and serene conclusion of the quest, which comes to which comes to us natrually and effortlessly – that is, if we relax and allow it to come to us. That is, if we relax and allow it to come to us.

The first chapter overviews this effortless acceptance approach and the intuitive means that naturally bring it to us.

The final chapter of this key takes an entertaining "flip trip" approach to illustrating the importance of making space in our lives to accept and receive the gifts.

Intuition, Not Effort

Trying to march down the healing path will leave us unsatisfied and unchanged; we must allow our mind to do what it intuitively knows how to do.

The next few weeks were a bit turbulent, filled with the highs of insights and self-discovery and the lows of uncovering additional layers of pain. Some experiences were accompanied by periods of confusion, denial, and incredulity at what was revealed. Some included emotional suffering, with shouting and frustration, and a few sweet moments of clarity, peace, and calmness.

I was confronting and disrupting many of the old stories – particularly those of my domestication – that were so firmly entrenched in my life outlook. Particularly encouraging was my growing ability to observe and identify the stories and victim dead-ends. My wife logged many long hours as my sounding board, idea-reflector, and insight-clarifier.

But I was impatient to move more quickly, to just get through it and be done with it. I worried that with all the time it was taking, important things in my life would still languish, and I'd lose the opportunity for significant accomplishment and relationships.

Finally, the day for our next meeting arrived. After a brief chit-chat, I shared with Brad a summary of my activities and progress over the past few weeks. "I'm actually encouraged by the progress and insights, but it seems so slow, like such baby steps. It almost feels like it doesn't stick – like I have it figured out, but then find myself a few steps back, dealing with the same issues next time it comes up.

"I really need to get these things resolved soon, Brad. It's a huge drag on my career, my relationship with my wife and my overall life direction."

Brad thought for a moment, leaned forward and said, You really like to horriblize the future, don't you?

"What do you mean, horriblize the future?" I asked.

Well, as I listen to you talk, I hear you project into the future, and imagine everything awful that could go horribly wrong.

"Well, maybe. But I'm just trying to be realistic about what I see the probable outcomes are."

Okay, but might it not be just as probable that things could turn out much better than you imagine? Isn't it possible that events come into your life that you haven't even considered, that turn out to take you in positive directions, or perhaps open new opportunities that aren't even in your current frame of reference?

"Well, I hadn't thought about that. I guess it's possible, but it doesn't seem likely at this point."

Remember our discussion about linearity? Brad reminded me. Nothing actually happens in the past or the future. Anything that happens, or that you control and create, only happens in the present. The past and future are the dimensions of the linear world.

The present is the dimension of consciousness or awareness. It is also the sensory dimension. You are working on the healing process, which is a sensory process, but you are approaching it from the linear, or non-sensory, dimension.

Regretting the past and horriblizing the future keep you out of the present, out of the dimension where healing can be sensed and experienced.

"Remind me again of the sensory healing process," I replied, not wanting yet to acknowledge my less-than-effective efforts.

Sensing Healing

A few minutes ago, you mentioned that you had some things figured out. That may be part of your challenge with making it 'stick.' At the risk of oversimplifying the magnificent and powerful dynamics of the bran and mind, I suggest that while all of us can sense healing, it cannot be thought.

We Unconsciously Know How to Heal

The soul knows how to heal itself. The challenge is to silence the mind. The visionary Renaissance physician Paracelsus once said,

"Physicians should be a servant of nature, and not her enemy. He should guide and direct her in her struggle for life and not by unreasonable interference throw fresh obstacles in the way of recovery".[3]

Our thought process is what we think we know in terms of our attitudes and our beliefs about our environment. It's all very linear. But if we can shut off the mind and move into a sensory

SECTION 2 : INTUITION, NOT EFFORT

experience, we start tapping into the intelligence of the body, the intelligence that created the body, and the intelligence that created the pain in the body. As we do that, we also tune into what will heal it.

But it's beyond the cognitive function. It's at the sensory level. It's like knowing, but not knowing how you know it. You don't think it. You don't figure it out. You sense it.

In nature everything heals itself. We try interventions – pills, surgery, or other treatments which can be helpful, but if we get out of our own way and let it happen it will heal. The only thing that heals the body is the body. The only thing that heals the spirit is the spirit.

Brad concluded and sat back in his chair. So, I've got another homework assignment for you. And this is not a small task.

"Okay, I'm willing to listen," I replied hesitantly.

I invite you to go on a 'flip trip,' he offered.

"What's a flip trip?"

You get in the car and start driving. Each time you come to a major intersection, you flip a coin to decide which way you go. Then, you drive to the next major intersection or fork in the road, and flip again. You keep flipping and see where you end up in three days.

"Okay, I get the concept. But why a flip trip? Why now" I inquired.

Besides horriblizing the future, not staying present, I sense that another challenge you are facing is efforting, Brad replied.

"Efforting?" I asked.

Remember that once you've moved into the pain and discovered its message, healing comes effortlessly and naturally. As I've been sharing with you today, it's not something you think, figure out, or obtain by sheer will.

The cognitive level is aware of the pain, but it also has a whole set of beliefs about pain. For example, if you have the pain, and you have a belief about the pain – that it's bad, it's going to kill me, I don't want it – and you still have the pain, then you have moved into resistance. And resistance makes the pain worse.

On the other hand, if you have the same pain and you say, 'Wow, that pain is telling me something. I'd better pay attention to it,' you move into it. And you embrace it. Then you have no resistance, so you don't add suffering to the pain. In that process, the body naturally heals the pain - without effort, without forcing it.

In our healing journey, pain is mandatory. Suffering is optional.

You are taking all the right steps, bringing militant healing and willingness to the process, but you are so anxious to resolve it that you are trying to force answers and resolution by sheer willpower. The irony is that while commitment brings you to embrace the pain and stay committed to the process, healing comes as a surrender to, or acceptance of, the healing path that follows.

It's often an unexpected new insight or path, perhaps something you had misinterpreted or would never have seen or considered at your present level of consciousness. That's why you can't think about it or figure it out – because your present consciousness level is probably blind to the insight.

This trip will help you to overcome that tendency to try to heal. It will give you the opportunity to accept what comes and allow yourself to heal.

Okay, I'm willing to give the flip trip a whirl," I replied.

Good. Just go with it. Wherever the road leads. Whatever the accommodations. Whatever the experiences. Just accept it and look for the insights that may come. Meditate. Be mindful and present. Brad's eyes were hopeful and confident.

Before you leave, let me share one additional thought, Brad offered.

"What, flip trip two-for-one coupons?" I asked.

No, unfortunately, there are no short cuts on the healing journey, he chuckled. Instead, you might consider the following experience as a different way to think about the healing journey.

More than 20 years ago, a client of mine came to the cancer group having been diagnosed with metastatic breast cancer. She came with fear, anger, and plenty of resistance to the pain she was facing. Other members of the group accepted and supported her through those challenging initial days.

Through slowly accepting her journey, she became one of the 'ordinary' amazing people who come to understand the concept of surrender as it related to her own healing. She completed that healing miracle by helping a new, angry, scared member of the group who ultimately discovered a similar path. This woman now teaches inner city kids who have not done well in the traditional education system.

As part of a celebration for cancer group members and their families, this courageous woman wrote a poem for the occasion that beautifully captured her journey of transformation.

As we sat in our circle of safey
A new one came,
Angry and afraid.
We all smiled
With eyes of understanding,
For we too had been there.

We each told our story,
Unique, yet similar.
About our own anger and fear –
And then the change,
With all of us – the change.

We had faced the dragon – We had looked at death.
And with each other's help,
Had made the choice –
To live, to live until we died.

To live each moment fully aware,
Fully conscious.
To enjoy the sunrise and sunset.

SECTION 2 : INTUITION, NOT EFFORT

To relish each day,
For we may not have another.
We counted this a blessing.

And we had grown.
The meek ones now assertive.
Then came the week the new one said,
"I decided to live,
To live fully each day.
I put on my muu-muu
And my straw hat.
I skipped down the road and sang.
I ran my stick along the fence.
I picked the neighbor's flowers.
I have never felt such joy.
You know it's the best,
The best thing that has happened."

We rejoiced together.

I closed my notebook and took a long breath. "There's really no checklist or formula for all this, is there?" I asked rhetorically. "Paradox, willingness, pain, acceptance. It's a very personal saga."

That's the challenge and also the magnificence of the healing journey, Brad replied. Every gift and wound are unique to every unique individual. Understanding the key underlying concepts puts you on the path. From there, your choice, willingness, militant faith, and openness to sensory insight guide you to discover your own personal gifts and healing.

I gave Brad our usual man hug and headed for the door. "I'll let you know how the flip trip turns out," I called back.

Just make sure you leave enough time to get back from wherever you end up, Brad laughed as I left.

Notes From My Note Pad

The present is where things happen, are created; also the sensory dimension

Regretting the past and horriblizing the future are in the linear world = NOT staying present!

Healing is sensory; :. Can only happen in the present.

We can sense healing, but it can't be thought or figured out. You know, but don't know how you know. You just know.

If you're efforting, trying to force it, it won't happen

Actually, we too are nature

In nature everything heals itself. Interventions help; but if let it happen, it will heal.

The only thing that heals the body is the body.

The only thing that heals the spirit is spirit.

Committed to take a "flip trip." Not sure how this will go down....

SECTION 2 : INTUITION, NOT EFFORT

Quotes From My Quote Book

Everyone has a wound
Every wound has a gift
The deeper the wound,
the greater the gift
Pain is the portal
To unlocking
The Gift in the wound

"In our healing journey, pain is mandatory. Suffering is optional."

– C. Bradford Chappell

THE GIFT IN THE WOUND

Pictures From My Sketch Pad

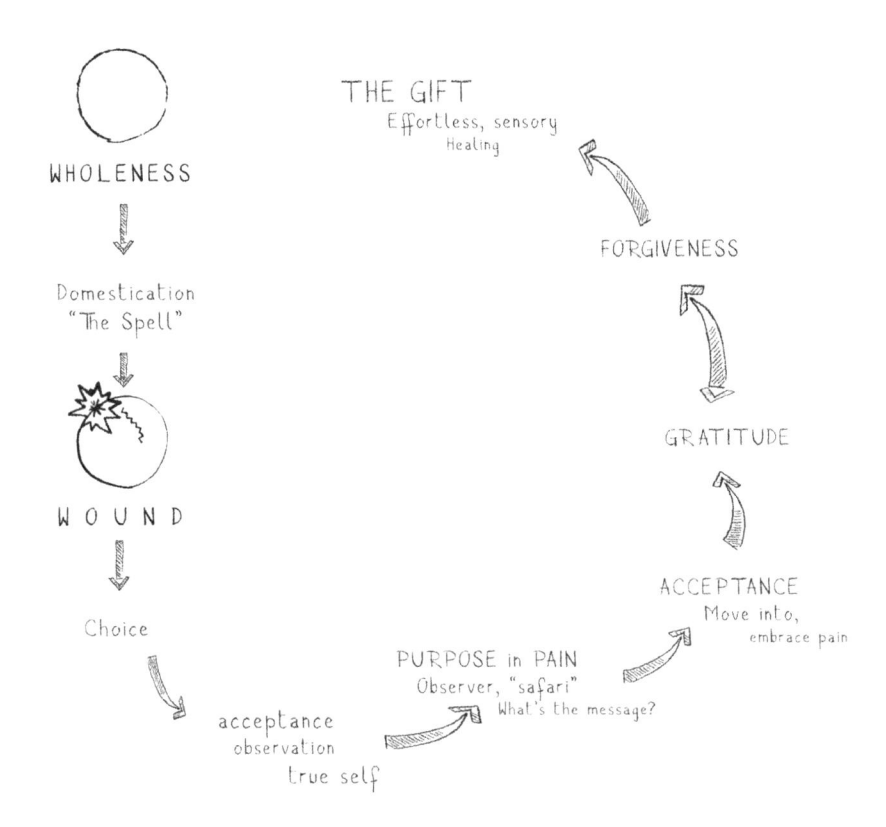

WHOLENESS

↓

Domestication
"The Spell"

↓

WOUND

↓

Choice

acceptance
observation
true self

PURPOSE in PAIN
Observer, "safari"
What's the message?

ACCEPTANCE
Move into,
embrace pain

GRATITUDE

FORGIVENESS

THE GIFT
Effortless, sensory
Healing

Create the Space

The Flip Trip

My wife Cynthia and I discussed the flip trip and designated a four-day window of time a few weeks out as the ideal opportunity to give it a whirl. At this point, my comfort level had increased to at least looking forward to the experience, but I was still a bit skeptical of the format and how it would turn out. Leaving things completely open to chance was a hard one to wrap my linear-focused brain around. My typical approach was to plan things out with a lot of structure, and then not deviate. I like a plan, and once I have a plan, it should be executed. Needless to say, I was moving way outside my comfort zone.

The morning of the trip finally arrived and we headed west toward the Interstate – our first decision point. For this flip, we designated heads as north, tails as south. As the entrance ramp approached Cynthia flipped the coin: it came up tails. I took a deep breath, looked at Cynthia, and veered toward the southbound entrance.

We traveled along for some time, discussing a number of the ideas we had both gleaned from our visits with Brad, and what this trip might mean to us personally and our relationship. I had hopes that it would be a time of inner discovery and healing, but honestly didn't know what to expect.

We soon came to the next crossroad – a major east/west highway. This flip, heads was west and tails was east. Cynthia flipped the coin: tails again. I took the eastbound ramp and we soon found ourselves gaining elevation and winding through beautiful mountain meadows and peaks.

A tee in the road required another north/south flip. We headed south this time. Over the next several hours our flips took us through small towns and wide expanses with sweeping vistas, until late afternoon found us in the Mesa Verde area of Colorado. This seemed like a great spot for our first night. We checked into a local motel and chalked up our first full day of flip-tripping.

Next morning, we got an early start and headed into the Mesa Verde Park itself. Our discussions intensified as we wound through the park and stopped for several side hikes to lookouts and walks through ancient Pueblo Indian ruins. There was something peacefully serene about this place, and I found myself enveloped in the Native American connection with nature and Spirit. In a way, time seemed temporarily suspended, particularly at one overlook with an unusually majestic vista. It was a chilly day, and the sunshine through the clear, crisp air warmed my back and cast a strong reddish glow to the canyon and cliffs before me. I felt a deep longing for the peace and serenity this place seemed to hold, and for a deeper, more honest connection with my life's companion by my side. I wondered what additional demons I would have to face to fulfill that desire.

I snapped back to my logical realm and realized that time actually was fleeting and we needed to get back on the road. We returned to the car, drove to the park entrance, and flipped. South once again. We wound through colorful red rock country and soon found ourselves in Northern New Mexico. The next flip took us east, and we were once more climbing up mountain passes through thickly wooded forests.

SECTION 2 : CREATE THE SPACE

We had decided to also make this trip a time of review and reflection, and so we brought along some of the more insightful books and references Brad had suggested. We spent several hours alternately listening to narration and discussing concepts that struck a chord, or a discord. As time passed, my feelings intensified, focused on the paradoxical burning desire for peace and resolution, and the frustration of painful paradigms that seemed to defy healing.

Flip, discuss, drive. Flip, discuss, drive. The winding path through cities, mountains, and valleys also wound through the sometimes-rocky terrain of relationships, misunderstandings, perceptions, and fears that uncovered old wounds and unresolved issues. I was beginning to wonder if this flip trip was actually going to flip me out for good.

Our flipping brought us into Santa Fe, NM long after nightfall. We found a nice dinner and hotel, and collapsed on the bed. And then it happened: total meltdown. My internal battle of ego vs. reality erupted in full force. The hard inner work I had undertaken over the past months, and particularly the last few days had called into question the domesticated version of reality my subconscious had built over many years. Now, in one last desperate effort to hang onto that version of the truth, the ego threw everything possible at maintaining the story.

In my mind, all the progress I had achieved was called into question. The insights and new understandings recently gained were now interrogated as imposters and invaders. Negative thoughts and self-talk doubted every new concept I was considering that exposed the fallacies of my domesticated worldview. How could I abandon these long-held beliefs and move to an alternate reality that was so foreign to how I had always perceived my situation and myself?

The further the subconscious led me down this path, the darker and more fruitless my efforts appeared. It seemed to me that my relationship and healing road had come to a pointless end, and there were no more branches, forks or flips available. I had no confidence that anything would ever really change, and things would keep blowing up and burning down. What was the point in going through all this? The mental anguish was excruciating.

Further talking. Much bla-bla-bla. Finally, exhaustion and sleep.

The next day I woke with clearer view of the battle that had been waged. I recognized that I was gaining ground, and that continuing to soldier on through these skirmishes was the path. I was determined to move into the pain that would take me to the next plateau. Besides, what did I have to lose at this point? We flipped: head West.

This time our path took us along the Pueblo Indian area in Central New Mexico. With a south flip we veered into more high country and Ponderosa forests. Around a bend, a sign seemed to jump out at us: *Cimarron Rose Bed and Breakfast*. After zooming past, we looked at each other, did a quick U-turn, and booked the last room available.

The next two days were filled with healing walks in the woods, hikes to lookout points, and solitary meditations in the pines. The experiences weren't without pain as I continued to face various demons and long-held beliefs. But I slowly began to recognize light dawning.

Amazingly, that light, that healing, became more and more effortless as the gifts were revealed in each painful issue and wound. It was just as Brad had described. Moving into the pain was excruciatingly hard – the last thing on earth I wanted to do. But the healing on the other side was effortless and spontaneous. I was beginning to feel more at home in this new "skin."

As the time to bid farewell to Cimarron Rose arrived, we marveled at how time had again seemed suspended in the healing flow. We pulled through the exit gate and stopped at the highway entrance. We looked at the coin, looked at each other, and laughed. No more flipping at this point – we actually did need to get home! I turned right and headed north for the first time in four days.

Shortly after returning home, another trip took us to Northern Arizona. We decided to incorporate elements of our successful flip trip, and spent several days at Sedona, Arizona and Zion Canyon, Utah.

Sedona provided opportunities for meditation and solitude along the rivers and canyons long sacred to Native American tribes. We also experienced the so-called "vortexes" of energy reported at various locations around the area. My personal meditation and solo time gave me opportunities to again practice mindfulness and connect with sensory healing input related to wounds I was still healing and working to understand each related gift.

The scene was repeated at Zion Canyon. Although a shorter stay, we found places of beauty and solitude conducive to healing practice. We found our commitment – our militant healing – rewarded with greater insight, impressions that guided our conversations, and raised consciousness that brought peace and tranquility to life and relationships.

As we returned, it struck me how similar our experiences had been at each location. And then this thought came: "It's not the place, it's the space." I realized that there was nothing particularly magical about Cimarron or Sedona or Zion. The key is that we had created space for healing where we were open to the effortless insights that lift consciousness and reveal life's greatest gifts. I felt, for the first time in over 10 years, grateful for my life, and grateful for this incredible opportunity given to me to move into my pain, and to let it heal.

SECTION 3
The Pool We Swim In: Return to Wholeness

Continuous Progress

Chapter 1 of the first section of this book set the foundation of wholeness as the starting point for each of us on this journey. We are not broken, in search of a fix. We are whole, with imperfect understanding or consciousness of that wholeness. We're in search of rediscovering our wholeness, much of which comes to us through understanding the gifts in our wounds.

This final section illuminates this amazing wholeness discovery that awaits each of us. After turning the five keys and walking the path, we have the opportunity of discovering that the pool we swim in was actually perfectly suited to our personal journey of discovery.

Return to Wholeness

Healing is to accept that we were always whole.

I couldn't wait for my next meeting with Brad. I had a lot to share regarding the trips and experiences I'd had in the weeks since our last meeting.

> So, how was the flip trip? he asked as we sat down. I see you got back home, so I assume you flipped a perfect circle – or you cheated at the end, he jabbed.

"Actually, the latter. Otherwise, we may still have been going in circles in New Mexico," I retorted. "But sincerely, the trip exceeded my expectations. It was an amazing, transformative experience."

I gave him a synopsis of our trips, highlighting the challenges and triumphs along the way. "I was especially struck that my greatest sensory insights and progress started to come after the darkest 'meltdown' night of the trip."

> I applaud your diligence in sticking with it and continuing to move into the pain, Brad replied.

As I related the final parts of the trip, I concluded with my most recent insight. "The flip trip is a brilliant idea, and the spontaneity led us to some truly remarkable places for my healing journey," I said. "But in retrospect, I realize that it wasn't the place, it was the space we created that enhanced the healing process."

> That's a great insight, Brad returned. As you discovered, just like the flip trip, sensory healing isn't something your think

about or plan or effort. As you create that space, you open yourself to the flow of Spirit, the effortless sensory experience that carries insights beyond what you can think. The flip trip gave you the opportunity to focus on and practice that sensory connection in a conducive setting. Now you can continue mindful practices that will provide a lifetime of growth in discovering the gifts in life's endless pain without having to always go on a trip or pilgrimage to a specific place.

"The other thing that struck me was that the healing felt so natural – like coming to a place that is totally familiar and comfortable," I added.

It's what we call the healing paradox, Brad replied. I could see him settle back for an explanation, so I opened my notepad.

The Healing Paradox: The Illusion of Something Lost

In the healing journey we often talk about finding wholeness, or returning to wholeness.

Remembering our wholeness, returning home, and returning to connectedness is the essence of the healing journey. A return to wholeness is not a return at all, but a recognition that we have been whole all along. It is a surrender to the reality of wholeness.

When we get quiet with ourselves, we start searching, and we sense a longing for something we believe we have lost. It's a longing that pulls us into examining ourselves – who we are. It may seem that the thing we have lost is somewhere in the past, when in fact it's a present state of consciousness that's incomplete. The paradox is, we think we have lost something when we really haven't, except in the ego mind. Many people spend whole lifetimes searching for something they haven't lost. But separateness is the illusion. The reality is wholeness, which is the truth.

It's not a return to a physical wholeness. Rather, it's a return to a sense of wholeness, that we're not somehow inherently defective, that we're perfect creations of a perfect universe, of a perfect God. These ideas resonate deeply at a basic level we really can't explain. Ultimately, they penetrate to the deepest personal level – into the heart. We have a longing to be ourselves and to be loved for who we are.

When we come to a higher state of consciousness, we discover we actually never lost connection. We always had it, but couldn't see it because we were looking through the eyes of the ego, rather than through the eyes of spirit.

I flipped back to my drawing page and drew another arrow from "The Gift" back to the starting point: "Wholeness." "So it really is like returning home, returning to where we started before being socialized or traumatized into thinking we were anything but whole."

> That's right, Brad replied. Reconnecting with our sensory knowledge of who we have always been requires that we also transcend those beliefs that aren't congruent with our true, genuine selves – beliefs adopted because of the domestication process.
>
> Essentially, in healing, we are remembering who we are. Some people call this the genuine self. This remembering allows us to shift our consciousness level and realize that we are perfectly

flawed beings with imperfect awareness of who we truly are.

That submission is a recognition that wholeness is not something you can think. It is something you sense. Shifting our consciousness is moving from one level of grace to another level of grace. Going from innocence to awareness, to complexity, to understanding, and coming back to this sensory experience of wholeness.

He leaned forward and stood, signaling the end of today's session. Ultimately, this is a journey of love: a journey of coming back to unity, of learning to love, of returning to love.

"You make it sound so simple," I said. "I'm going to need a couple of lifetimes to work through all this."

Not with the commitment and progress you've achieved, he replied. It will come to you exactly when and how you need it. Now you have eyes to better recognize it for what it is. In fact, I have a feeling that we won't be meeting as frequently any more.

"Why not?" I asked, a little puzzled.

You have progressed to a point that my advice may not help you as much, he said. My coaching is designed to start people on the healing journey. But my greatest value is more at the beginning of that quest. Once you reach a certain level of consciousness, you stay healthy and continue to progress by living the principles on your own – with occasional "check-ups" with me. It seems you're well on your way.

Emotion welled up in my throat. The thought of saying goodbye to close, frequent contact with my friend and mentor was totally out of the blue. "So, you're saying I'm healed… I'm whole?" I asked.

> Remember, that is the illusion. You were always whole. Now you know that you are whole. And as you keep reminding yourself of that, you will be able to stay on the healing path.

My mind was churning, rehearsing my progress at each step of the way of over the past months. My journey with Brad had been truly remarkable, but seemed as though it was just getting started. This coaching had become such a central fixture of my life, I had never stopped to ponder what came next. But the truth of what he suggested slowly starting to seep in. Like the flip trip, for example: I didn't have Brad by my side for the whole experience. I had followed the principles, leaned into the pain, learned its message, and raised my awareness all without his direct intervention. I had experienced a level of healing on my own in the face of very challenging emotional issues. Maybe I really could continue as my own guide and coach.

Gradually, a feeling of profound gratitude swelled up and squeezed out other thoughts, fears and doubts. Brad waited patiently as I processed.

Finally, I gave voice to the only thought that was left in my head. "Thank you, Brad." The words seemed so inadequate; a stark, simplistic contrast to the profound realizations that had spawned them.

> There is nothing to be thanked for, Mark. I only helped you realize what you already knew about yourself. So actually, you should be thanking yourself for your commitment to militant healing.

SECTION 3 : THE POOL WE SWIM IN: RETURN TO WHOLENESS

I looked into the eyes of my dear and trusted friend. The journey of returning to love which he had so carefully laid out for me over the months was now clearly personified in front of me through this wise, caring soul. I knew no amount of thanks could repay his experience, struggles and insights; nor his own mentors and teachers and the collective gift we enjoyed. A piece of his legacy had now passed on. I could only hope to some day pay it forward to another prepared student struggling in the journey's starting gate.

"So, no homework assignments this time?" I asked, hoping to lighten the mood a bit. "Didn't you teach me that 'when the student is ready, the homework appears?'"

Brad laughed as we headed toward the door. "No, that's not quite how I remember it. I think it's, 'When the homework is due, the dog appears.'"

We laughed, exchanged man-hugs, and said our goodbyes. As I walked across the office entry, I paused in front of the picture of the butterfly metamorphosis I was introduced to on my first visit, and had often passed on my way back to Brad's office. As I stood and gazed at the phases depicted in the maturing process, I was drawn to the fully emerged butterfly on the far right-hand side. The intricate beauty of the colors and patterns on the wings highlighted the magnificence of the majestic creature that so starkly contrasted with the small, greyish cocoon in the middle. The adult perched confidently in its full splendor, almost triumphantly, as if to say, "I am all those things, but this is my true magnificent self."

I shook my head. What a fight. What a journey. What a change. What an astonishing transformation.

I took one last look at the butterfly, glanced over at the safety of

Brad's office door, and quickly strode out into the light of the day.

Notes From My Note Pad

In healing we are remembering who we are = the genuine self.

Requires that we transcend beliefs not true to our genuine selves – adopted through the domestication process

Shift our consciousness level, realize we are perfectly flawed beings with imperfect awareness and understanding of who we truly are.

The healing paradox:

We think we've lost something, see ourselves as separate from everything

A longing for something we believe we have lost.

But separateness is the illusion. The reality is wholeness

The paradox: we've only lost something in the ego mind

People spend whole lifetimes searching for something they haven't lost!

We have a longing to be ourselves and to be loved for who we are.

Come to a higher state of consciousness, discover never lost connection.

The key: willingness to examine ourselves, ask the hard questions

Militant willingness to walk through the pain of this world.

Our mistakes = our greatest tutors, if we don't shame ourselves for our humanness.

Quotes From My Quote Book

"Essentially, in healing we are remembering who we are."

– C. Bradford Chappell

THE GIFT IN THE WOUND

Pictures From My Sketch Pad

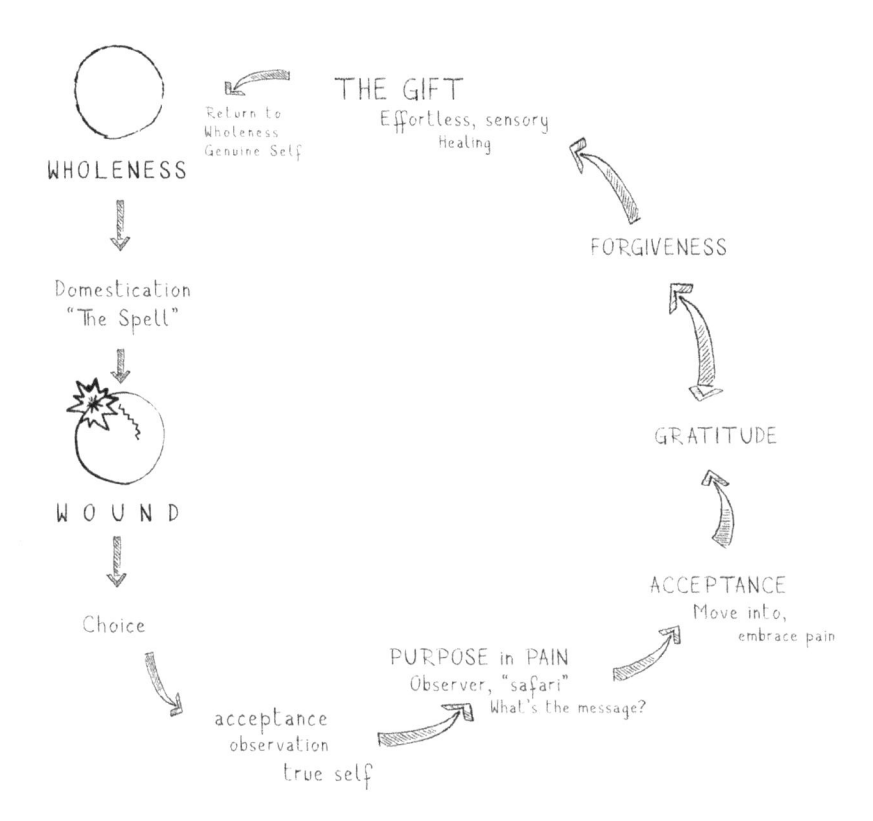

WHOLENESS
Return to Wholeness
Genuine Self

THE GIFT
Effortless, sensory Healing

Domestication "The Spell"

FORGIVENESS

WOUND

GRATITUDE

Choice

ACCEPTANCE
Move into, embrace pain

PURPOSE in PAIN
Observer, "safari"
What's the message?

acceptance
observation
true self

199

EPILOGUE
The Gift

EPILOGUE : THE GIFT

Brad's office wasn't far from my house, so on a particularly warm, sunny morning I decided to walk rather than drive the car over to visit my friend. As I turned down the tree-lined lane along the route, a flood of memories and impressions filled my mind.

I realized this was the very spot where a few years earlier my wife Cynthia had given me the "If you're not in, I'm out," talk that had changed the course of my life. That day I was a walking time bomb, filled with fear that I would lose my marriage, my livelihood, my home, my family – everything that was important to me. I could see no way forward and no way out other than to keep slogging through.

Those first few meetings were so strange and painful to me. Brad was asking me about things that were so far out of my frame of reference they seemed to be a foreign language. Choice, paradox, domestication, victim. Such alien concepts and experiences. And yet, at some level they resonated deeply. It was like walking through a fog and recognizing shadowy outlines that somehow drew me in and beckoned me to move on despite the confusion.

I reflected on the overwhelming relief and hope that swept over me as I first sensed his sincere belief that I wasn't broken and needing to be fixed, but that I was a perfect human being with imperfect consciousness and understanding. I thought of when, early on, Brad looked me in the eye and said, "You know, this is the perfect experience for you." What a ridiculous idea!

Like most everything else we discussed, his assertion proved to be right. The depth of my wound brought me to the teacher, and to the point of willingness to listen and learn. It was the perfect motivator to set up the perfect healing journey.

I glanced down at the notebook I carried under my arm. That trusty tome chronicled my visits with Brad, and my journey of becoming more fully awake. Each time we met, I had eagerly jotted down new insights, concepts and understanding that seemed to pop out of our conversation and find their way onto the page. Impressions and images became pictures and maps that illustrated a lively story of discovery.

Each new concept opened a world of understanding and hope, and cracked the door for small steps of progress toward finding meaning in my often-meaningless world. In the process, I confronted searing pain that tested my resolve to discover the insight each carried, and abandon the easy way out of adding each to my already swollen library of victim bla-bla-bla stories.

Instead, I had re-written my life, chapter by pain-filled chapter.

I had wrestled with the demons of my own multi-generational domestication and recognized the judgment I was putting on them in defining my life.

I had escaped a number of deeply embedded victim stories and sparked my way into militant faith, gratitude, and forgiveness.

I had even become the teacher in sharing my insights, pictures, and maps of the healing journey.

And I had found myself full-circle, back to wholeness. Back to genuine me. Back to something I thought I had lost, but didn't have eyes for.

As I continued my walk down the lane, it struck me how really, nothing had changed. The people, places, circumstances around me were all still the same. And yet, *everything* had changed. Far from cursing life for my circumstances, I saw each new day as a gift, and each new wound as an opportunity to learn, to grow, and to change. I saw the world with new eyes of understanding, gratitude, forgiveness, and joy.

My wounding had led me to the teacher, and the teacher had led me back to me. To whole me. To conscious, more fully awake me. To joyful me.

As Brad always said, life is pain. But therein lies the secret to self-discovery, wisdom, and joy.

To those who are willing to embrace it, discover it, and sense it, the gift is in the wound.

AFTERWORD
Wound to the Head

AFTERWORD : WOUND TO THE HEAD

The call from Brad came in on Wednesday morning. We often met on Thursday mornings, and it wasn't unusual for one of us to call the day before if there was a conflict that required a schedule change.

Hi Mark. I'm not going to be able to meet tomorrow morning, Brad said after I picked up the call. No problem, I thought. We'll just reschedule for a later time. I'm going in for emergency surgery on Friday, Brad continued.

"Emergency surgery?" I asked, dumbfounded.

They've found a large tumor in my brain that requires immediate operation, Brad clarified.

I was stunned. For one speechless minute my mind went through all the worst-case scenarios of what might happen to my dear friend during or after surgery. "Any details on type or extent of the tumor?" I asked anxiously.

We won't know the extent or exact prognosis until they have gone in and assessed or removed the tumor, Brad replied.

"I see. What can I do to help?" I enquired.

Nothing right now. I'll let you know as things progress.

"Ok. You're in my prayers, my friend," I replied.

Great. Thanks.

That was it. I hung up with my mind racing a thousand different directions.

Two years earlier, Brad started having trouble with his vision. He was losing peripheral vision as well as depth perception. He consulted with three different eye doctors, had surgery to repair his macula, but still continued to have problems. In December he showed me a new pair of glasses he was trying in order to deal with the challenge. His eyesight was getting bad enough that driving was becoming dangerous for him and others. By January, for his own safety he had his wife start driving him where he needed to go. At the end of January, a friend finally convinced him to get an MRI. The results showed a large tumor that covered almost a quarter of his brain.

Not a wonder he was scheduled for surgery two days later.

There were many tense hours and days as Brad progressed from surgery, to ICU, to continued recovery in a hospital room. When I visited him there, I was amazed at his rapid progress. Only a few days following such a major procedure he was alert, sitting up in bed and conversing clearly and lucidly. His doctors were equally impressed with the speed of his healing. The tumor had been successfully removed with no apparent major side effects. The surgeon related that the tumor was literally millimeters away from blocking a major vessel that feeds the brain. Had it grown much larger, a major stroke was inevitable.

Over the weeks that followed, Brad continued to improve, regaining his eyesight and gradually returning to a graduated work schedule.

I was anxious for his health, but as I saw him return more and more to seemingly normal life, I found myself more anxious to hear the impressions and insights of this wise teacher who had suddenly become the student of his own teachings and counsel. Brad was finally feeling well enough to share some of his thoughts.

AFTERWORD : WOUND TO THE HEAD

"I'd really appreciate hearing some of the insights you gained as a result of your cancer experience," I began when we were again sitting face-to-face in his office.

After all these years of counseling and facilitating the cancer group, I was finally called on to practice what I had been preaching, he said. A principle I have taught over the years is that we are accountable for how we choose to see any given event that occurs to us. I was not accountable for the diagnosis, but I was accountable for how I dealt with it. So I chose to see this as an opportunity to engage in the healing process. But since this procedure involved more people than just me, I wanted to involve them, too.

As each healthcare professional came in to attend me, I gave each an invitation. I invited them to see me as more than just the diagnosis or procedure. I invited them to see me as a person who wanted to be a partner in my procedure. I asked them to help me help them in attending to me. I did this from the person who shaved my head to the surgeon and nurses who cut into my skull. I had a conversation with the anesthesiologist and told him that the only thing I could do for him was to hold him in my prayers. He took my face in his hands and told me I was in his prayers as well and that he would take good care of me. All of the anxiety that I had in previous hours flowed from my mind and my body and I experienced perfect peace.

The last thing I recall before losing consciousness was my wife saying, 'I'll see you on the other side.' I remember thinking, 'Other side of what?'

Well, one of the first things I remember in the recovery room was saying to my wife, 'Are we on the other side?' Brad chuckled.

While in the ICU I had some experiences that almost convinced me that I had travelled to the other side.

The night after my surgery ended, I suddenly woke up from a deep sleep. I looked over at the door of my room and was terrified to see a black figure standing in the doorway, completely blocking out any light from behind. Remembering that fear, like pain, is just a messenger, I got control of my wits enough to realize that, terrifying as this creature was, it really couldn't do anything to me. I had just undergone a surgery where they took my skull off, and I suspected that this being would do nothing worse than that. Resigned to that thought, I invited it in. It stooped through the doorway and lumbered over to the side of my bed. It stood there, menacing and powerful. Again bridling my fears, I asked it if it had a message for me. To my surprise, the second the words were out of my mouth, this creature began to shrink. It got smaller and smaller until it had gone below the side of my bed. Leaning over, I watched as it shrunk to the size of a child, then scurried off.

No sooner had this little devil disappeared did waves of beings of light begin flooding the room. My mind was filled with clarity and inspiration, and among other thoughts I realized that we all are so perfectly flawed. Every creature that comes into mortality is perfectly flawed in some way. As humans we are socialized that flaws are something we must hide or deny. It became so very clear to me that it is our flaws that perfect us. As we recognize and embrace our flaws it gives us opportunity to grow and to evolve. It gives us opportunity to discover our genuine, authentic selves. Hiding our flaws through shame causes so many of today's emotional and psychological problems.

AFTERWORD : WOUND TO THE HEAD

As we come to embrace our flaws, we are then more able to embrace others as flawed. If we are able to be vulnerable enough to embrace our flaws and we find people of like mind, we then are able to heal and to assist in healing the planet.

"That sounds a lot like embracing our pain," I volunteered.

Yes it is, Brad continued. This is a never-ending story. No matter how enlightened you are, life is going to be painful. From birth to death, life is painful, no matter what stage. If you surrender, that pain becomes joy, a sense of serenity. If you embrace the ultimate painful experience, your own death, as I just did, you find that you have also embraced the fullness of life. There is no fear; only peace, serenity, and unspeakable joy. It's a joy that defies description. You don't know how you know it, but you know it. You sense it with everything in your being. The gift is in added light and knowledge, grace, purpose of life, and consciousness.

He stopped and contemplated for a moment. The goal is to die well. To look back fondly on your life with not a lot of regret. That means looking back at your whole life: the losses, mistakes, missteps, and disasters, as well as what we define as successes.

Looking back over my life I again realized that everything in this universe matters. Everything. Successes, failures, mistakes, triumphs, disappointments – they all matter. Everything has purpose. The consciousness of how we view each one of them is the defining element that puts meaning on all the experiences in our lives. It's the defining element of whether we will find the gift in the wound, or merely focus on the wound. The key is our willingness to examine ourselves – our level of consciousness – and be willing to consider another possibility, another way of viewing our experiences in life.

The dilemma we have is that's not the consciousness we typically swim in. We stay on the linear dimension and rarely access the vertical, sensory dimension. When one of our ideas resonates with the truth of the universe, it's a sensory experience. In theology, we call that The Spirit or harmony.

When people hear it, and they have done this work, it always feels familiar. You feel like, 'I know that.' It's not thinking-true, its sensory-true.

In a psychological world there are ways of knowing. We can know by reason, we can know by scientific experiment, we can know by experience. But there is another way of knowing: We know, but we don't know how we know. That's the sensory experience. That's the spiritual experience. That's the deeper knowing.

I could tell Brad was tiring. His thinking, clarity and insight were as sharp as before the surgery, but he was still getting his physical stamina back. I closed my notebook. "I so appreciate this time together. I'm grateful that you are still with us," I said, "so I can keep discovering the gifts my life has to offer."

Brad smiled back. Progressing to that point is like dying before you die. You discover the depth and meaning of your life's experience without actually dying.

But the true gift is that these principles always work, over and over. They transcend time, mortality, race, culture – all linear constructs we've created. It is possible to heal. There truly is a gift in every wound – in every life experience.

AFTERWORD : WOUND TO THE HEAD

I stood and embraced my wise friend – something a few weeks ago I was unsure I would have the opportunity to do again in this life. I basked in the warmth of his spirit and courage for a moment, and then took a step back.

"So what's the prognosis?" I asked. I didn't want to think of losing this treasured relationship in my life, but I wasn't oblivious to the reality of his situation.

> Well, they say they got it all. But you know how cancer goes. We'll just have to watch the quarterly checkups and see what shows up. If it's clear after a year, the outlook is pretty positive. If not, there will be another gift to discover.

"So, where do you go from here?" I asked.

> With what's served me well over my life. While there have been times where I wondered if the 'dark night' would end, overall I have deep gratitude for my relationships and the experiences I have had. Very early in my life one of my favorite scriptures was found in Ecclesiastes 1:17-18, 'And I gave my heart to know wisdom, and to know madness and folly: I perceived that this also is vexation of spirit. For in much wisdom is grief, and he that increaseth knowledge increaseth sorrow.' I might add, to know sorrow one must also have known joy.

Brad's next appointment had just arrived. I walked to the door and smiled as he waved and said, "Be good."

Just like old times. I wondered how much longer this friend, mentor, and teacher would be on my journey with me. I felt that he might not be long for this world. But though the teacher had become a student, I felt certain that countless generations would be blessed to have his wisdom as a guide on the path to healing, on the path to peace, on the path to finding their gift in the wound.

Notes From My Note Pad

Enlist others in your healing

We are perfectly flawed. Our flaws perfect us if we embrace them

Surrender becomes joy, serenity

Die before you die

Deep knowing = sensing. You just know, know that you know

This stuff always works – over and over. Teacher or student.

APPENDIX

APPENDIX : BIBLIOGRAPHY

Bibliography

1. https://www.quora.com/
How-many-grains-of-sand-are-there-in-a-handful-of-sand

2. https://biblehub.com/matthew/22-21.htm

3. *Time, Space, and the Mind*; Irving Olye, Celestial Arts, 1977 pg. 21.

About Mark L. Dayton

Mark L. Dayton is an author, mentor, business executive and entrepreneur. He combines a passion for understanding the keys to human healing and wholeness with a knack for clear, engaging communication to provide narrative and mentoring that helps countless individuals move forward in life.

Inspiration for this book is drawn from his multi-year journey from deep depression to wholeness and joy, and highlights his firm belief in the power of the mentor-mentee relationship.

His career includes executive positions with companies from Fortune 100 to startups, and spans multiple industries and locations. More recently he is involved in suicide prevention humanitarian organizations and education.

Co-author of *The Phase 3 Fulcrum* and numerous articles and guides, Mark resides in Salt Lake City where he enjoys frequent mountain retreats for biking, skiing and writing inspiration.

About C. Bradford Chappell, PhD

Brad Chappell has worked with people in the healing process for over thirty years. He believes that while some things cannot be cured, there is nothing that can't be healed. This approach has helped countless individuals find meaning and direction in life through a wide variety of challenging circumstances.

He was an early innovator in creating cancer support groups for patients dealing with adverse cancer diagnoses. He still actively runs a group based on the original approach that augments hope and healing for a wide variety of cancer patients. Diagnosed with cancer himself, Brad continues to practice the principles of healing.

Brad holds a PhD in Social Psychology and Family Studies, and maintains an active practice, Transformations Accountable Life Coaching, LLC. Brad is an avid outdoorsman and horseman, and relishes time away at his ranch in the mountains of Central Utah.

Made in the USA
Monee, IL
19 October 2020